GLYN RHYS

———

WERE THOSE THE DAYS?

Events a Surgeon Can't Forget

First impression—2003

ISBN 1 84323 319 3

Printed in Wales at
Gomer Press, Llandysul, Ceredigion SA44 4QL

I Ann

ACKNOWLEDGEMENTS

Without embarrassing them by naming them, I here convey my thanks to the many friends who have suggested I record some of my experiences.

To Dr R. Brinley Jones, President of the National Library of Wales, to Miss Gwerfyl Pierce Jones and her staff at the Welsh Books Council and to Mr John Lewis of Gomer Press, I offer my sincere thanks for much help and advice.

As a confirmed technophobe I am also grateful to Mrs Sheila Thompson for her computer skills in transcribing my written word.

CONTENTS

FOREWORD

There are those who know the author of this collection as a man whose medical career was distinguished. Those who know him better also recognise the kind, sympathetic observer of human nature and the eye for an interesting incident. But those who know him *really* well will acknowledge Rhys the superb raconteur – stylish, observant, understanding, humorous, serious, sensitive – who shapes words with the skill with which he once wielded the surgeon's knife: the governmental reports of the MOH have given way to carefully planned paragraphs. The result is a splendid collection, varied in subject-matter – compelling, elegant, and a great pleasure and privilege to read.

Dr R. Brinley Jones, CBE FSA
President,
The National Library of Wales

RIDING

The word 'riding' seems to have different meanings for different people, at different times, at different stages of life and in different ages.

The first memory I myself have of riding, is sitting astride my father's shoulders while he jogged me around the house as a special treat before bedtime, my mother protesting that she'd never get me to sleep after so much excitement. I must have been about two years old.

The next memory I have of riding is of being wheeled in a pushchair by an aunt. I was probably about three years of age. Riding along happily on the flat, wide pavement of a main road, I was safe in my pushchair, garden hedges on one side, the roadside kerb on the other. Still wheeling along in the same direction the pushchair suddenly jerked down over the kerb, and I was being wheeled straight across the mouth of a minor road, which plunged down steeply on my left. It was the brink of a precipice and I was strapped into my pushchair teetering helplessly on the edge of a sheer drop. Terrified, I screamed loudly and jolted the pushchair back and forth so violently it almost overturned, precipitating me down into the abyss, which was the very thing I was terrified might happen. Vaguely I remember my aunt scolding me, but I was quite incapable of explaining the cause of my terror. Even now I shrink from steep slopes, but have usually been able to conceal this phobia – unlike my arachnophobia.

As a daring four-year-old I rode around and about the garden on my trike with the red wooden seat. The motive power came from the thrust of my feet on the pedals which stuck out, like bent yellow arms with black rubber palms, from the centre of the large, red, rubber-rimmed front wheel. I must have expended a tremendous amount of energy, rapidly flexing and extending first one leg, then the other, as I careered around the crazy-paved garden paths. I was under strict instructions not to venture beyond the garden gates, so of course I did. It was a Saturday morning and I rode my trike to a nearby house where I'd heard there was a large goldfish pond. It was summertime and after failing to catch a goldfish with my bare hands, I turned my attention to the rose garden with its various scents and colours. I had managed to snap off quite a few rose-heads to give my mother, who always had fresh flowers around the house, when I was apprehended by the man and wife who lived there. The blooms were snatched from my hands and I was unceremoniously marched to their front gates, which were very firmly clanged shut after I had been escorted out with my trike. I still recall the surprise and indignation I felt. I had resolved to say nothing of my morning's escapade, but when I arrived home I found I had been missed and was obliged to give an account of myself. My mother immediately took me to the goldfish-house whose childless owners apparently won competitions with their prize roses. I was perplexed that my mother made me apologize, because I knew she loved flowers, but I started blubbering when the pretty lady of the goldfish and roses gave me a goldfish and a sweet. However, when we got home, my mother surprised me by saying I'd been stealing and gave me a terrible row and sent me to bed after a smack-bottom. I still remember that the real hurt was due to the fact that the nanny had not been sent out of the room while I was being spanked.

A few months later I was again perplexed by my mother's odd reaction, when once more I disobeyed orders not to go outside the gates, which by now had been fitted with a child-proof lock. I was using stones I had found in the garden to build a house for my cat 'Tinks', but the walls kept falling down because the stones were so irregular in shape that I couldn't get them to fit together. However, while being taken to kindergarten in the mornings, I had noticed a pile of bricks which would fit together and would be ideal for Tinks' house. So after tea, I hoisted my trike and myself over the garden wall, and pedalled purposefully the hundred yards or so down to the heap of bricks. I managed to get two bricks onto the seat of my trike, which I then wheeled back up the road, lifted the bricks onto the wall and pushed them into the garden. After climbing back with my trike, I wheeled the bricks to a nook behind the potting shed, which I had decided would be the site for Tinks' house. I was leaving with my two bricks after my third foray, when a rough, bull-necked, hairy workman who was building a people-house bellowed at me, "If I ketch yer liddle bugger darn 'ere agen, you'll 'ave my big toe up yer arse!" I had not heard grown-ups shouting before, and I ran home very frightened.

"Mam, what is 'liddle bugger' and what does 'arse' mean?"

I could see my mother was shocked.

"Where did you hear those words?"

"Down there," I said, pointing, "where they're making a house for Dr Newgate."

"Who said them?"

"A big furry man, like the big bear in 'Goldilocks', only he was smelly."

"What were you doing?"

"Nothing!" I bleated, because the cat-house was a secret between me and Tinks.

Knowing, as all parents do, when their small child is lying, she persisted. At last I had to tell her about the bricks and the house, and take her to see the six bricks

13

lying in the small plot I had cleared. My black and white cat followed, tail erect.

"You were very naughty to take those bricks," said my mother, "but that man had no business to speak to you like that. He's an uncouth labourer."

"What's uncouth?" I piped.

"It just means he's not a nice man – someone you wouldn't ask to tea," she said soothingly, plying me with cake and lemonade. I knew then I wouldn't be smacked and, looking back, I suppose my mother was trying to make me forget my original questions.

But I too could be persistent and kept asking, "But what did he mean?" Wisely my mother made light of it and said, "Oh! He just meant he would kick your bottom, but in this house we never use nasty, rude words like that fellow and don't you ever let me hear you using them! And anyway, only cowards kick anyone."

"Mam, what's a coward?" – and so it went on; but in any event the bricks disappeared, and two days later, a dog kennel was delivered and placed on my chosen site.

When I was about five years old, I remember riding in my father's bull-nosed Morris Cowley car, which had a dicky behind. One day my mother asked my father to stop and give a lift to two prim-looking ladies she knew, who were hurrying along the pavement. With urbane expressions of gratitude they got up into the dicky-seat and off we went. Suddenly there was a cloudburst and, being rather quaint ladies, they opened their dainty, flowered umbrellas which immediately turned inside out. Timidly they tapped on the back of the hood and my father stopped the car. After he had snapped their umbrellas back into shape, they thanked him graciously, saying they would be drier walking. As they toddled off down the road, I recall my father laughing heartily and saying, "Intelligence isn't synonymous with common sense." Though I didn't understand what he meant, I joined in and started giggling. But I certainly did understand what my mother meant when she said, looking pointedly at me, "It's rude to laugh at other people's bad luck," though I noticed she herself was smiling.

Another car episode occurred a year or so later when, for company, my father took me to pick up his rather intimidating spinster sister, who was coming to stay with us. She was wearing a huge hat with a long multicoloured feather which kept waving around, and as I tried to grab it she said, "If you don't behave yourself you'll be put in the dicky-seat."

"Not a good idea," said my father. "Too dangerous for a child. But leave your auntie's feather alone, that's a good boy."

Hearing me called a 'good boy' was too much for my aunt. "There's not much room in this car," she grumbled and, condescending to speak to me, "If you sat on my lap there'd be more room."

I had by now taken a dislike to her and so refused. We rode along in silence. Suddenly there was a loud thud. Turning to my father she demanded, "What was that noise? You must have hit something. You're driving too fast."

"Nonsense," said my father.

But some people on the pavement were waving and laughing and pointing behind us, so my father stopped and we looked back down the road. It was festooned with a trail of corsets, embroidered nightgowns, baggy white bloomers, jewellery and some things that looked like the liberty bodices I wore – only much bigger; at the end of the trail, near the car, was my aunt's large leather suitcase, wide open.

I could feel the tension as my aunt said indignantly, "You left my suitcase on the running board, you fathead!"

I really hated her now for daring to call my father

names, and I nearly whooped with delight when my father told her, "If you'd had a grain of common sense, you'd have fastened your case properly."

He got down from the car and gathered up the spoils, helped eagerly by laughing children. I was just about to join in the fun when my aunt forcibly restrained me saying, "Oh no you don't, sonny-jim," which I thought was really stupid, because my name wasn't 'Jim', and I certainly wasn't her son.

We rode home in complete silence and my aunt disappeared upstairs to her room. My mother sent me to wash my hands. I soon got back to the breakfast room and found my parents falling about with laughter, and so I joined in although I didn't really know what we were laughing about.

I was ten years old and had been pestering my parents for a year to give me a bicycle, but without success. So it was perhaps fortunate that somehow it got to my parents' ears that I had been seen riding my pal's bicycle at speed, down a steep hill, with my arms spread out horizontally like wings. To my mind I was skilfully avoiding traffic on the road by guiding the bike with a combination of swivelling on the saddle, leaning my body to left or right and flapping my 'wings' as the occasion arose, without, of course, any recourse to the handlebars. As a result I was made to promise not to borrow anyone's bike again, and having kept that promise for six months, I was given my first bicycle on my eleventh birthday. However, I continued performing bicycle-acrobatics and within a few weeks had broken my arm, which was set at home and immobilized in wooden splints and a sling. Next day I had an X-ray at a friend's house and in two days was back in school. However, my broken arm did not protect me from being slippered for talking in class, while quietly telling a friend all about it, during a maths lesson.

Graduating two years later to a superior, three-speed dynohub bicycle, complete with gear-case, my friends and I used to compete in daredevil bike races, usually after dark. We called these races 'shanks'. During the day we would have chosen a tortuous undulating ride a few miles long through the oak woods, the clearings serving as passing places. These furiously contested shanks invariably resulted in a few falls, and on one occasion a broken leg. The first to complete the course was dubbed the 'champion shanker', whose prize was to choose the next course.

Our school was for boys only, and sometimes, by secret arrangement, we'd ride our bikes out to those same oak woods to meet schoolgirls of our own age, and show off our tree-climbing skills. These clandestine meetings gradually superseded our shanking competitions as the prizes to be won began to appeal more and more. The boy who climbed the highest within a given time was allowed to claim the girl of his choice as his prize. She had to sit on his crossbar and be taken deep into the woods to hide. Five minutes later each of the remaining boys would capture a girl, lift her squealing onto his crossbar, and set off in search of the first pair who, by now, would have discarded the bike and run to hide up an oak tree. The girl would usually need the boy's help to unhitch errant twigs from her blouse or skirt, as they climbed higher and higher to hide entwined in the branches. If the girl refused to climb, they'd have to hide in the undergrowth. Riding home alone one evening after one such innocent outing, I began for the very first time to feel the rare thrill of a wonderfully overwhelming sense of elation. In that first flush of euphoria I climbed into bed and, in my sleep, it all became an ecstatic dream.

★   ★   ★

It was at the time I was riding my trike during my fifth year that I was first placed bareback astride Doll, one of my uncle's plough-horses, and I soon became attuned to the firm, but gentle, slow plod of that gigantic animal. A few weeks later, having gained too much confidence, I put a milking stool on top of the mounting-block and clambered onto the horse's back. But I had made a mistake; it was not Doll – it was Flower, a frisky member of my uncle's plough team, and Flower decided to trot. Trotting without saddle, stirrups or reins, I soon fell off and, hearing me yell, my uncle appeared and did the correct thing – he put me straight back on Flower. He led us to the stables and made me promise not to mount a horse alone again. Over the years I came to regard Doll and Flower as among my best pals and, since then, have admired everything about horses – their noble bearing, their power and their independent nature.

As a child my cheeks burned red with tears as I read, and re-read, Anna Sewell's book *Black Beauty*. No one has ever done more for the humane treatment of that most noble of animals, the horse. When I was in my twenties I made a pilgrimage to Lammas in Norfolk. After much searching, I found Anna's simple tombstone hidden in the long grass of the small Quaker graveyard there. Her book lives, but she is all but forgotten.

In my very early teens most of my summers were spent with my parents at the seaside, and I knew they weren't at all happy with what I did there. I had found out that the owner of some stables near the sea was called Jac Patric, and that he was looking for a stableboy. He also owned the Black Lion hotel, later to become well-known as a haunt of Dylan Thomas. I wasted no time in tracking down the owner. I found him in the stables grooming one of the horses and immediately applied for the job of stableboy and was taken on. The result was that instead of whiling away my time on the beach, I spent each morning in the stables as an unpaid stableboy. The arrangement we had was that if I mucked-out, fed and groomed the three horses during the mornings, I could ride them during the afternoons and evenings. I soon discovered that it was better for the horses if I took it upon myself to attend to them last thing at night as well, because after a day at the bar, my employer tended to be rather fuddled as he lurched around the stables. In any event he seemed only too happy to be relieved of these duties. To me it was a sheer delight to look after them, and the horses and I got to know one another better and better as those glorious weeks of summer drifted by.

The Arab and the cob had been gelded and the hunter was a mare about seven years old. All three had been trained. The Arab was a 15 hands grey about five years old with a long silky mane and tail. He was light-framed with a deep chest and was graceful, docile and intelligent. Lady, the hunter, was a beautiful 16 hands 2 inches chestnut and was reputed to be a thoroughbred that had been ridden to hounds. She had good lean muscular shoulders that sloped well back from the point of the shoulder to the withers and also had a deep chest. She had large eyes with a good width between them and the forelegs were strong with short cannon bones. Though capped, the hocks were sound and the pasterns were not too sloping nor too long. She was high-spirited but when she became accustomed to my handling her, her nervousness to some extent disappeared. The cob was a blue roan just 13 hands 3 inches high and at least 12 years old. He had a well-shaped head with a powerful neck, and was sturdy and stocky with short strong legs. His conformation was that of a first class cob and to cap it all he was calm, kind and reliable.

There was no harness room and only two snaffle bridles; one fitted the cob and the other, with adjustments, could be made to fit both the Arab and Lady. Because the Arab had a smaller head the cheek straps had to be shortened, so that the ends of the jointed bit just touched the upper parts of the lips on either side without wrinkling them when the reins were slack. These adjustments to fit the length of the Arab's head also allowed the headpiece and noseband to sit comfortably. The throatlash had to be tightened and the browband slid into the correct position, while the buckle on the noseband had also to be tightened so as to encircle the Arab's nose and lower jaw comfortably. Lady did not like being bridled, but a little treacle smeared on the bit made things easier. There were also only two saddles, one for the cob and the other, though it sat well on Lady, needed a numnah under it to make it fit the Arab and prevent a sore back or even a saddle sore. The stirrup irons on the larger saddle were the correct size for me but the bow of the cob stirrup irons was too narrow, so I used those from the larger saddle.

Once, some years previously, I had mounted a horse and cantered off almost immediately after girthing up, and soon found myself flat on my back, the saddle having slipped round underneath the horse. Since most horses breathe in deeply, enlarging their chests while being girthed up, this taught me to check the girth a few minutes after saddling up and before mounting.

It was a privilege to look after those noble animals who soon got to know my voice – maybe because it was so different from JP's rasping whisky voice. I already knew that riding-horses are naturally highly strung and sensitive and respond to gentleness, kindness and affection. I think it was because they became accustomed to my voice and touch in the stables that they responded so well when I rode them. Whenever one of them was taken to a horse show I always chose to travel in the horsebox, but I was never allowed to show, because I was only the stable lad, and anyway I refused to wear a hat. Though a horse could kill a man, he is by nature a timid animal but can display great courage if he knows his rider and has confidence in him.

I spent hours in the saddle every day during those long summers riding each of the three horses in turn. The Arab and cob responded to light hands, but the hunter was not so tractable, and I guessed that injudicious use of hands and arms when riding sometime in the past had, to some extent, spoilt her mouth, gait and temper. I'm afraid I made myself unpopular galloping at full pelt over the two-mile stretch of firm golden yellow sand, terrifying the supine sun worshippers shamelessly exposing their repulsive white beer-bellies. Though there was never an accident, I was nevertheless reported to Jac Patric, who owned both the Arab and the cob, for tearing along the country lanes and also for jumping Lady over high hedges when riding cross-country. Lady was a natural jumper and once, when I lost control of her at a fast gallop on the beach, we sailed up and over a disgustingly enormous upturned mountain of a belly, which wobbled like a jellyfish on springs. JP's reply to these complaints was that his horses needed to be exercised, and that anyway the hunter was not his horse, but he was merely stabling her for the local Member of Parliament who could easily be contacted at the House of Commons. Nothing came of it. Later I discovered that on the rare occasions the MP rode Lady, he had her hobbled! JP's only advice to me regarding the complaints was, "When you're posting along on a blood horse avoid the hoi polloi!"

Though I seemed to have satisfied Jac Patric that I had a working knowledge of horsemanship, and knew

21

something about the advantages and disadvantages of the forward seat and backward seat in cross-country jumping, there was some information I wanted from him. Among other points, I needed to know the different alphabet or language that each of the three horses understood. This was because there seemed to be a subtle difference in the response to the same instruction, given by my hands, legs, heels or voice, in each of them. Also I wanted to know if any of them had been trained to expect the rider to rise to a particular diagonal at the trot, and whether any of them had been schooled in changing the leading leg at the canter.

"How the devil d'you know about fancy things like that?" he croaked in his thick, rusty voice.

With a certain inappropriate hauteur I told him, "I've studied Zoöpraxography."

"What in the hell is that?" he growled.

"It's the science of animals in motion," I explained.

Had I been older and more worldly-wise I'd surely have realized he must have been getting pretty exasperated with the young whipper snapper who was questioning him.

He was not at all impressed, and grunted as I followed him into one of the bars of his hotel to get the key of the stables. It was in fact only the second time I had ever been in any bar, the first being during my entomological period when I had caused much amusement among the topers, when I had asked for 'a pint and a half of stale ale'.

"You're under age my lad," said the barman sizing me up in my white open-necked shirt and khaki shorts, "come back in six years and I'll serve you."

"Wha d'ju wan wiv shtale beer, boy?" slurred a purple-faced man so enormous that he completely enveloped the bar stool that must have been under him.

"I mix it with black treacle and paint it on tree trunks at dusk to attract moths," I piped.

"To attract women more like!" gurgled a large chap with a shining red face, "Give it to the kid, barman, and I'll pay."

Wondering why the whole bar was laughing and guffawing, I rushed out, red with embarrassment, clutching a large, uncorked bottle full of evil-smelling, dark brown liquid, which I promptly spilt on a Persian rug in a hallway at home. I remember my father asking why the place smelt like a cheap sawdust bar. No one knew. I was not even suspected. The rug disappeared that evening. So did the smell.

To me the heady smell of a horse's coat is a bouquet of nostalgia. Nothing can ever approach the pure feeling of freedom and exhilaration, flying through the countryside, soaring over hedges and ditches, horse's mane and rider's hair streaming in the wind.

In my early adolescent mind I knew that only girls and sissies wore riding hats and jackets. My long-suffering parents had already provided me with riding breeches, because I believed that no serious rider wore jodhpurs, which were only for children and novices. However, I had to wait a few years before my parents gave me riding boots. So passed those seemingly endless happy days of summers long ago.

Sadly, all those golden, cloudless days ended abruptly one evening when I was in my late teens. Jac Patric had been drinking heavily all day, and that evening told me I had not cleaned the mud and dried sweat from the Arab's coat before giving the bran and linseed mash, and neither had I thoroughly dried and wisped him before rugging up. This was completely untrue as I was meticulous in my attention to stable management and told him so. He became very aggressive and brought his riding crop down with a sharp cut across the Arab's muzzle causing the poor horse to scream out. Next, though very unsteady on his feet, he challenged me to a fight. Even if he had been sober I would not have hit him because I knew he would take it out on the horses. That was the end.

But very many years later, when I called to see him in an old people's home, he and I shared a dram.

Quite apart from being a summer stableboy, I used to seize every opportunity that presented itself to indulge my passion for horse-riding. Fortunately I had a cousin, Pat, whose father owned many horses and ponies. Our mutual grandfather had won his spurs as a splendid horseman, even though he did not take up riding until early middle age, and then only on the advice of his medically qualified brother, who, on a visit from Wisconsin, had diagnosed him as 'liverish'. Pat was an attractive girl who rode side-saddle, and we spent as much time together as we could, riding her father's horses when we were home on holidays. Some of them were so unschooled that I felt I should be wearing a judo black belt, so adept did I become in being thrown and recovering to regain control. She persuaded me to try riding side-saddle but I found it most unnerving and was quite unable to retain my seat.

One winter's day, trotting along a ride in the woods, I was looking over my shoulder saying something to Pat, when I received a violent blow on the side of my head and was thrown heavily to the ground. I was momentarily stunned, and when I came to I found I was lying face down unable to get up. Vivid mental images of a broken back and a wheelchair flashed across my mind, while the heartless laughter of bovine blockheads flooded my ears and echoed through the woods. It took a few seconds for me to realize that there was no one there except Pat, and that she was shaking with helpless laughter – and I soon joined in. It was a ludicrous situation. I had not been looking where I was going and had been struck across the side of my head by a stout tree branch. I could not get up because my horse, bless him, had stopped immediately I was thrown. He was standing guard over my prostrate body, his hooves planted firmly on my hacking jacket, which Pat had insisted I wore, and which had been thrown wide open as I flew through the air.

Unfortunately, over the years our horse-riding holidays became more and more infrequent, as Pat became more and more interested in boys.

But luckily through the good offices of a girl I knew, I had for many years had access to a fine 17 hands 1 inch crossbred hunter. He went under the name of Jaffa because his sire was reputed to have been a splendid steeplechaser called Orange Prince. It was Jaffa who had carried me in my first fox-hunt where I underwent the disgusting initiation of being blooded; this confirmed me in my resolve never to hunt again. So once again I became a solitary rider. At the gallop he was a racehorse, at the canter an armchair, but he was averse to trotting or walking. Jaffa was a fearless, even impetuous, jumper and at take-off packed a tremendous punch with his hindquarters. So long as I played my part by leaning forward, seat just off the saddle, gripping with the knees with heels well down in the stirrups to maintain balance, he never once unseated me at any jump. However, since a hatless acquaintance of mine had sustained a fractured skull on being thrown from a horse when jumping, I had taken to wearing a steel-reinforced black bowler hat.

Some years later, on a bitingly cold February day after prolonged and heavy rains and snowfalls, I learnt more about Jaffa's versatility – albeit against my will. After an exhilarating two-mile gallop across the fields, soaring over gates and hedges, which, over the years, I had learnt were free of stakes and barbed wire, we arrived at the village common. We made our way to a pool which was a still backwater of the river. Jaffa was in the habit of standing up to his knees in this pool and drinking as much as he needed – but not today. As soon as he entered the water he was up to his withers and I was up to my crotch in icy cold water. I should have realized that the river was in full flood, but before I could turn Jaffa around onto dry land, he had struck out into the black fast-flowing waters of the wide river. It was my first experience of being astride a swimming horse, and I imagine it was Jaffa's first experience of swimming. He held his head twisted acutely to one side, so that it was almost horizontal. I realized that this was in order to keep his nostrils just above the level of the dark menacing waters so that he could breathe. As his body rose and fell in time with his powerful strokes, I found myself alternately up to my waist, then just before the next stroke suddenly plunged down up to my chin, in the piercingly freezing waters. The angry river rushing past us in full spate was carrying great chunks of ice down from the mountains. It was a painful and unnerving experience to be thumped in the chest, and almost jolted out of the saddle by one of these huge, fast-moving blocks of ice. We were about a third of the way across, but the irresistible flow of the vast volumes of floodwater was carrying us down to where the river narrowed between high craggy banks and, gathering momentum at an alarming rate, surged thundering under the bridge. Though we had probably been in the river for only a few minutes, a small crowd had already gathered on the bridge and on the opposite bank. It must have been an amazing sight – a boy in a black bowler and white mac astride a gigantic horse, being borne relentlessly towards an ugly death in the rapids, watched by a body of helpless onlookers. Someone even slung us a hopeless rope. In trepidation, trembling with cold, I thrust my feet right home into the stirrup-irons and gripped as hard as I could with my knees. I knew that if I slid out of the saddle into the treacherous waters, I would be sucked down into the freezing black depths by my heavy water-logged clothes, and then of course one kick from Jaffa's thrashing hooves would finish me off anyway.

There was only one course of action: in desperation I tugged cruelly at the left-hand rein, and managed to direct his twisted head diagonally upstream towards the opposite bank, urging him on with voice and heels. He responded magnificently and, snorting violently, gasping in convulsive spasms, he struck out with great power. Even so, the merciless headlong rush of the unforgiving river was still sweeping us nearer and nearer to the horror of the rapids awaiting us under the bridge, echoing there in a booming crescendo of crashing water that was already drowning out the shouts of the onlookers. I feel now that Jaffa must have sensed his end was near, and that without me on his back he would stand a far better chance of swimming to safety, but nevertheless he did not attempt to unseat me – that would have been my end. Struggling heroically against the malevolent, dark swirling river he managed to reach the bank just a few yards from the hungry, surging waters under the bridge. He dragged himself up the riverbank a few yards, only to collapse on the footpath and fall inanimate onto his side. While, in a dazed state, I was trying to extricate myself from under him, a bewildering confusion of voices seemed to be floating down, as if from far away:

'He's burst his heart, poor horse.'

. . . 'Never seen such cruelty.'

'Disgraceful – report him to the RSPCA.'

. . . 'Should be ashamed of himself.'

'Get the police.'

. . . 'Ask the vet to finish him off quick.'

'And the boy as well.'

Numb with cold, staggering and trembling as though in the throes of the ague, I tried to rub his chest where I thought his heart was. Quite suddenly, without any warning, Jaffa was on his feet shaking himself. I did what I knew he expected me to do. I remounted him. The crowd scattered and gasped as, snorting like a dragon, the wonderful horse clattered up the long flight of stone steps which took us onto the road that crossed the bridge, and before I could rein him in he was cantering through the village.

We soon arrived back at the stables and, after staling, Jaffa had his gruel with some water and hay while he was being dried. Once he had been cleaned of mud and sweat he relished his bran and linseed mash. He was rugged up with body, ears and legs dry and warm, and before going home I made sure he had plenty of bedding and a final feed of corn.

As I was stroking his forehead and flicking his forelock, I chucked him under the chin and thanked him for saving my life. He nuzzled into my chest and whinnied softly as I said goodbye. I didn't know it, but that was the last time I was to see Jaffa. Three days later, hearing the foxhounds baying, he jumped a hedge to join the hunt and was staked in the stifle. He bled to death. I had lost a faithful and incomparable pal.

Sometimes, when I'm half awake or dozing by the fire, I think I can hear a gentle whinnying nearby. I get up and go to the windows and look out across the fields, but then I realize I've been dreaming.

THE MUMMY

If you happen to go into a cowshed at the seventh stroke of midnight on Christmas Eve, you will see the cows standing up to their udders in warm birth-blood. It was our red-headed Sunday school Superintendent who told us this, and he said it was a deep, deep secret. As members of the junior class learning about the Old Testament, we promised not to tell. Anyway my parents wouldn't have understood because they didn't go to Sunday school. The only one I might possibly have considered telling about this extraordinary phenomenon would have been Santa Claus, because he would have known more than anyone else about the wonderful and mysterious events that occurred on Christmas Eve.

One Sunday we had a lesson on Abraham, the father of the Jews, and soon afterwards I went with my parents on a visit to my Uncle Griff, who lived way out in a beautiful part of the country in a house called Machpelah. I was very surprised that he didn't seem to know what I was talking about when I asked him if he would show me where Abraham and his wife Sarah were buried, and also – showing off my recently acquired knowledge – Isaac and Rebecca and Jacob and Leah. He didn't even know that they were all buried in a cave in a field on his land at Machpelah. The Sunday school Superintendent had told us; so it had to be true. My father explained that they were buried in a foreign land, in a place called Hebron near the Dead Sea which he showed me on my Bible map.

Not until I was an adolescent did I learn from my friend Dilys, who was older than me, that our respective nannies used to meet each morning to gossip,

29

while they wheeled us around and about in a huge cemetery – so large one could lose one's way in it – just like Père Lachaise. This early initiation may have been responsible for the morbid fascination that obsequies performed in different cultures held for me later. In any event those morning airings were probably the cause of my pricking up my seven-year-old ears when the Superintendent, no doubt thinking we needed background information, started telling us about the embalming of Jacob called Israel. He must have got carried away, because he then went on to tell us, in some detail, about the methods and rituals practised in the long-drawn-out and complicated processes involved in the embalming of the pharaohs. His descriptions were so vivid that two of the girls had to leave the vestry to be sick. But we boys were tough, and wallowed in the graphic details of how a cruel hook was rammed right up inside the pharaoh's nose and twisted around inside his skull to mash up his brain, which then oozed out of his nostrils like collops of slimy snot. The insides were pulled out through a cut in the belly and stored in four special jars. He told us how the body was soaked in a solution of salt and baking soda for thirty-five days and then rubbed with oils and myrrh and wrapped in miles of bandages smeared with gum. At the end of seventy days it had become a mummy and was laid in a gold coffin inside wooden and stone coffins. I remember one of the cleverer boys asking him why they didn't use frankincense as well and I was surprised he didn't seem to know the answer, because he changed the subject straight away and told us about the Book of the Dead. It was then that I decided to read this book when I grew up.

We learnt too that, although the ancient Egyptians were good painters and could make statues, they never painted or made statues of their naked slaves because that would have been rude. This set our immature minds racing and we eyed the girls who were sitting apart on their own benches. I recall feeling vaguely uncomfortable, the same as I had felt a few weeks previously, when Hilda, who was two years older, told my best pal David and me that we were dirty-minded little boys. She had caught up with us on the way home from school, and found us gawping up at a bedroom window, where a girl of our own age was standing stark naked on a table, right up against the window. She was smiling at us over her left shoulder before she turned round to face us, still smiling. This must have fired up David and me, because a little later we caught up with Hilda and her retinue of younger girls and, quite suddenly, there on the pavement, we pulled Natalie's navy knickers down to see if her bum was as nice and white as the one we'd been drooling over in the window. Hilda said that if Natalie's father didn't come round to our houses and tell our parents, then *she* would; but we heard no more. However, Hilda must have been jealous of Natalie and the window-girl, because of what happened soon afterwards when I was confined to my bedroom convalescing from chickenpox. Her mother had called to see my mother and had sent Hilda up to play with me. That afternoon Hilda did such rude things that afterwards she made me look through my bedroom window at the Cathedral while I had to swear 'across my heart and hope to die', that I would never tell anyone about what she had done – and I haven't.

I also have to thank the Sunday school Superintendent for laying the foundation of what I have found to be one of the most effective ways of ridding oneself of a bore at a party. One informs her (occasionally him) in an offhand manner that the reason one was late arriving at the party was that, as a qualified embalmer, one had

had a call to embalm a body as a matter of urgency. If this does not get rid of the tiresome individual, one can then proceed to describe the six-point injection method of embalming. If the limpet still clings, one is then entitled to launch into a description of the difficulties encountered in embalming a body after a post-mortem examination. In this case the corpse has to be reopened for each organ to be removed, punctured and treated, before being returned to the respective body cavity. Meanwhile the body has been drained and the six-point injection method completed. Assuming the bore has not yet left, a vivid description of the embalming procedure after a thorough medicolegal post-mortem examination performed overseas would be the next step. This can be topped off by a graphic account of the embalming of a putrefying corpse; this is guaranteed to send the bore to the lavatory to vomit and one is then free to socialize with those of one's own choosing.

Be that as it may, to return to the Sunday school. One thing I did tell my parents, was that the Superintendent of the Sunday school had told us that if we really wanted to know how the Egyptians lived during the days of the Old Testament, we should ask our parents to take us to see a film called *The Mummy*, which was currently being shown at a local cinema. My parents were frequent theatre-goers and very occasionally I was allowed to go with them, but I could not recall them ever going to see a talking picture. No doubt thinking it was an educational film, they readily agreed to take me. I certainly had never been inside a picture-house before and had no idea what to expect. I was overawed by the sheer size of the edifice, which to my mind lived up to its name 'The Pavilion Super Cinema'. I could hardly believe my parents when they told me that it had been built on what had been a roller-skating rink, where years ago they used to dance

32

away the hours until late into the night, because to me this was a palace that had always been here, and would last forever.

While my father bought the tickets I stood in the foyer entranced by the coloured fairy lights; it was just like Christmas and I felt warm and cosy. As we went through the green double-doors into the dark picture-house, I wondered why the girl standing there tore the tickets in half because my father had only just bought them. I thought she was very wasteful and when she asked my parents if I was with them, although it was plain to see I was, I knew she was stupid as well.

Then the silly girl asked me, "How old are you, my lovely?"

When I said, "Seven and three quarters," she giggled, as soppy girls do.

But when she patted me on the head I just hated her. My parents were following another girl who had a torch, and she was dopey as well, because after she'd asked if we wanted to sit together, she put us to sit behind two huge men and a woman with a big hat, so I couldn't see the picture-screen. After she'd gone with her flashlight to lead some other people into daft seats, my father moved us further along the row, so that I could see the pictures on the screen because the seat in front of me was empty. When I got used to the dark and looked around, I saw that we were sitting in the centre of a huge room as big as my school hall. But here we were comfortable in springy seats, not standing up crammed like sardines as we were in assembly listening to old Guv Jones booming away. There were moving pictures of men standing on platforms and shouting at crowds of people who were cheering and shouting back, and people flying around in aeroplanes, and soldiers marching about all over the place. This went on for ages and I started fidgeting.

My mother, sensing I was getting bored said, "The picture about Egypt won't be long now. They're showing us all the latest news first."

"Why can't everyone buy newspapers like us?" I cheeped up.

"Shush! Quiet!" said my father. Then it got a bit more interesting when they showed lions and tigers running about, and monkeys scratching themselves and jumping up and down in trees. "That's Whipsnade," said my father.

"What's that?" I asked.

"Shush!" said my mother.

Soon the lights came on and some huge red curtains closed over the screen. My mother said it was all right to talk now because it was an interval – like playtime in school. A pretty girl with a tray fixed in front of her tummy with a sort of harness came round trying to sell ice cream from the tray. My father bought me one but it didn't taste nearly as nice as the ice cream in the school tuckshop. I had noticed there were no other children in the cinema, and began to wish I'd asked David to come but he didn't go to Sunday school, and Ronnie didn't go to my Sunday school because he was a Roman Catholic. The lights started to go dim and before it went dark again I tried to finish my chocolate ice cream, but in my hurry a lot of it fell down onto the front of my shorts and made a sticky mess. My mother gave me a hanky and told me to rub it off.

The curtains opened and the first thing I saw was a name in big letters and it filled the screen – the name was 'Boris Karloff'.

My father leant towards me and whispered confidentially, "His real name is 'Pratt' and he plays cricket."

This set me off giggling and I said in my piping voice, "Well he must be a real prat!"

But a chorus of 'hushes' made me hunch up in my seat and keep quiet. Anyway with funny names like that I guessed he must be an Egyptian who was good at cricket; in fact he was the Mummy himself and was called Imhotep in the picture. But he wasn't a real mummy because they had bandaged him up alive and hadn't taken his insides out. Then one of the men found a roll of old paper and read some magic words out of it. When the mummy heard the words he opened one eye and then the other. He very slowly unfolded his arms and that tore the bandages. Then he took the paper from the man who started laughing and screaming like a fool because he was very frightened, and when he saw the mummy walking out of the room he went raving mad. It was quite scary and my mother asked me if I wanted to go home but I said, "No, I'm not a scaredy-cat. It's wizzo!" Imhotep then went to a museum and knelt on the floor, just like I did every night to say my prayers, but he didn't ask God to make him a good boy. He kept saying "Ank – san – aam" slowly over and over again and he wasn't kneeling by the side of a bed. He was kneeling by the side of the mummy of a pretty girl whose name was Anksanaam and she had been a princess in ancient Egypt. He told her his own name, "Imhotep", a few times and then kept on reciting very slowly like they do in church:

"Ank – san – aam," . . . "Ank – san – aam."

The creepy music got louder and louder and his awful old face came nearer and nearer as it got bigger and bigger until it filled the screen. I thought he was going to jump out at me and I shrank back in my seat. My mother caught hold of my hand and half got up saying, "Come on, we're going."

I raised my treble voice in protest, "No, I'm not going. I want to stay."

Some people sitting nearby started getting irritated and 'shushing' and rather than create a scene my mother sat down, but I was glad she kept hold of my hand.

Imhotep tried to make the princess get up by reading the magic words from the old roll of paper, but it didn't work because her guts and stuff had been taken out and put in the four jars, so he gave up.

After a bit he found a live girl called Helen who looked exactly like Anksanaam. But she told him she liked a boy called Frank who lived a few miles away. This made Imhotep very cross and he lifted his hand up; on one finger was a magic ring with a huge stone in it and on the stone was a picture like a beetle. He pointed the beetle to where Frank was, and Frank fainted off when the rays from the magic beetle hit him, although he was miles away.

Then Imhotep's face filled the screen again and his huge, nasty eyes were staring out straight at me, but I knew it was only a picture and I felt in my pocket for an aniseed ball. I crunched it up. Imhotep then made horrid eyes at Helen and she went to sleep. She dreamt she saw Imhotep at Anksanaam's funeral in ancient Egypt. He was crying like a baby and said he was going to miss her a lot. He told Helen she had to take Anksanaam's place and he was going to kill her and turn her into a mummy. But he promised not to take her insides out, so that when he read the magic words she would get up and be a living mummy like him and they would be together for ever and ever. Helen was lying on her back and Imhotep had his dagger out ready to kill her, but she managed to slip out of her dream and wake up. She told him she didn't want to stay with him. Then she went on her knees in front of a big statue of an Egyptian god. He sent lightning to strike Imhotep who burnt to ashes with his piece of paper so Helen was free. She went to Frank and they kissed and cuddled which was soppy and spoilt it all.

It was getting dark when we came out of the pictures. My parents were whispering to one another and I heard the words, 'unsuitable', 'should have left', 'he didn't want to'. Then my father said two words out loud, 'culpably irresponsible' but I didn't know what he meant. My mother put her arm around me and said I deserved a treat. They took me to Gethin's Dairy, where I had my favourite meal of baked beans on toast and strawberry ice cream. This was great because I was never allowed tinned food at home because it was unhealthy. My mother had once bought some beans and tried to make them into baked beans, but it didn't work out and I wouldn't eat them. But she did make scrumptious ice cream.

When we got home I was allowed to stay up late and listen to some funny people telling jokes on the wireless and we played a few games of 'Pit'. I wondered why my parents were being nicer than usual to me. My father showed me some trick moves on the chess board, and my mother didn't tell me off for dirtying my shorts in the pictures with all that chocolate ice cream. Then they went and asked me if I wanted to sleep in their bedroom – of course I didn't – I wasn't a baby. After I'd got into my pyjamas and said my prayers, I climbed up into my big bed. My mother gave me two bedtime stories instead of only one and got all soft kissing me good night. I was surprised when my father came up to my bedroom to say good night because he always said 'good night, sleep tight' downstairs. When they'd gone I got down from my bed and pulled back the curtains so that I could look out over the roof that sloped away down under the windows. In the clear brittle light my gaze wandered down the winding steps through the rockery and I saw my tent on the lawn. The stream that ran alongside the vegetable garden sparkled in the moonlight. Beyond the garden lay the field where David and I played; it seemed to be bathed in a strange, shimmering silver light. In the distance were the floodlit Cathedral and the twinkling lights of the town below. I wondered why ships were blowing their foghorns because it was such a clear night. They sounded so sad, but perhaps they were lonely and were just doing it to keep one another company. After a bit I felt sleepy and crept back into bed.

In the distance I thought I could hear my uncle chanting in his spooky vicar-voice,

"Ank – san – aam," . . . "Ank – san – aam."

It was getting louder and louder.

"Ank – san – aam," . . . "Ank – san – aam."

It kept on and on, getting nearer and nearer. Why was my mother looking through one of the open windows and calling me? Why was my father trying to get out of another window in his pyjamas? He couldn't make it because my mother went and pulled him back. Then they started arguing and I heard my mother saying, "You'll frighten him and he'll fall off the roof."

"I'll go out through the French windows and catch him," my father shouted. I felt strangely uneasy. I was flustered and shy that they had caught me. I was on my knees trying to wake Natalie up. She was all white and navy and sleeping on her tummy. My secret was out. What would they say? She was Helen and she was Anksanaam and I was myself and I was Imhotep; and it was me chanting:

"Ank – san – aam," . . . "Ank – san – aam."

Then Addy the maid came to the window and I heard my mother telling her to put some clothes on and go and help my father catch me. I didn't want to be caught. Why couldn't they leave me alone with my white and navy girl? She was still sleeping and looked very nice. Why couldn't she hear me calling her?

"Ank – san – aam," . . . "Ank – san – aam."

There were no jars around. No one had touched her insides. Why didn't she wake up? Something white was moving towards me. Her bottom part came nearer and then her top part. She was rolling over and over and smiling at me over her left shoulder as she came right down to me. We touched and then we were floating and falling:

"Ank – san – aam" . . .

"Anksanaam be damned!" swore my father. I was lying in his arms.

"Are you awake now my lovely?" asked Addy, stroking my hair. My mother came rushing through the French windows looking very white.

They took me up to their own bedroom and closed the windows. Addy brought me some milk and chocolate biscuits and they all made a silly fuss of me. My mother said something about a horrid nightmare. I didn't tell them it was a lovely dream.

Next day I saw Natalie. She ran away and I went to play in the field with David and Ronnie.

The next Sunday there was a new Sunday school Superintendent.

It was nostalgia that took me back to the Pavilion Super Cinema many years later. The building was indeed still there, but its imposing façade and canopied entrance had lost all their bright colours. The whole structure was dreary and uninviting. Maybe that is why, uninvited, I pushed my way into the decaying foyer. The broken box office still announced that the balcony seats cost three shillings and sixpence. The mysterious doors into the cinema hung on their rusty hinges, their green baize torn and mildewed. Through the doors I found the secret wooden stairway to the projection room, but the stairs were crumbling with dry rot. Risking broken limbs I climbed up through the musty, fungal-smelling air to the seclusion of the dank little projection room hung with a latticework of cobwebs. I looked out and down through the projection windows. The gloom of the auditorium was pierced by shafts of sunlight which shone down like spotlights through gaps in the broken ceiling. The narrow sunbeams were reflected from the still, smooth surface of the magic silver screen, now torn and draped face-up across the dilapidated seats. I had seen enough. Sadly I stole out of that place of long-forgotten dreams.

Today a petrol station stands on the graveyard of my memories.

ALICE ET AL

David and I were cousins and we were best pals. Although he was nearly a year older than me, we were in the same class all through primary school. Even when he had to go away to boarding school we remained friends. I was an only child but he had a sister about seven years older. There was another only child on the scene – a girl called Hilda who was two years older than me and whose parents were very friendly with my parents. She used to call for David on the way to school and they'd both call for me. More often than not other girls would join us on the mile walk to school, but there were no other boys going our way, so we usually ended up as a tight knot of seven- to ten-year-olds, with David and me the two loose ends straggling behind.

None of us had a watch, but quite suddenly Hilda would raise her voice and start running, "Quick, we're late!" and the whole knot would come undone as she bawled out, "Guv Jones'll be mad!" We believed her because Guv Jones and Hilda's mother were great friends.

At this David and I would stop swapping cigarette cards of sporting heroes and, to show we were boys, would race past the girls. Hilda was a fast mover and anyway had had a good head start, but soon one of us boys would pass her.

As soon as she saw she was no longer leading the pack, she'd stop running, stand tall on the pavement, hands on hips, crying out in the sing-song, high pitched voice which was always used to call the younger members of a gang together, "All in! All in! All in!"

Breathless, the girls would cluster around her awaiting further instructions, while David and I would saunter nonchalantly ahead hitching up our light grey shorts and tightening our elastic, red and black, snake-clasp schoolboy belts.

While trying to keep up with the rest, perhaps one of the smaller girls would have tripped up on an uneven flagstone and graze her knee and start blubbering. It was then that I would come into my own, because Hilda turned a horrid shade of pale green when she saw blood. David would kneel on one knee and get the girl to sit on his thigh. I would then ask the girl, who probably would be about my own age, to give me her hanky; often this would be a major procedure, and she'd jump up and hide behind Hilda, who would stand arms akimbo glowering at us, while the wounded girl would put her hand up her skirt and yank out her hanky from under the elastic of her knickers and present it to me. Being a girl's hanky it would often have needlework pictures of flowers or small birds in different colours in one of the corners, so I would select a plain corner and tell the girl to put it in her mouth and wet it with spit. Occasionally she would shake her head, protesting through her sobs, though I didn't realize it was probably because of where the hanky had been. But when I made as if to put it in my mouth, I was surprised at the alacrity with which she'd snatch it from me and stuff it into her own mouth. In the meantime Hilda would have pulled the hem of the girl's skirt down almost to the knee and, looking away, would hold it firmly in place while I gently teased the dirt out of the abrasion and pressed until it stopped oozing blood.

The operation completed we would race away to school until suddenly Hilda would call a halt, because she'd seen Blanec the bogeyman hiding in a gateway and, led by Hilda, we would chant in our piping voices, "Ol' Guv Jones, broke 'er bones, tumblin' over cherry stones," in order to make Blanec go away.

This accomplished, we would tear off to school and disperse to our different classrooms to register before being shepherded by our various teachers to the main hall. We would stand there in rows and fidget and shuffle around and whisper to one another, until ol' Guv Jones herself, in a black cloak with a scarlet lining, would sweep into the hall for all the world as though she'd just got off her broomstick. Everyone knew she was weird and a pall of silence would fall upon the hall as, in a deep voice, she demanded even more silence.

One Saturday morning Hilda's father took Hilda and me out fishing on a river and he caught some trout. When we got back to Hilda's house he said, "Well, my boy, d'you know how to clean a fish?"

"Wash it with soap and water," I ventured.

"Not quite. Come into the kitchen and I'll show you."

"Are you coming too, Hilda?" I asked somewhat timidly.

"No. It's horrible; I'm going up to my bedroom to take my wet things off."

I think I would have preferred to have gone up with Hilda but I didn't want to show I was afraid, so I followed her father into the kitchen.

He was a big man with a big voice and he said with relish, "First of all you chop off his head and tail, see!" and he suited the action to the words.

"Then you slit him open with a sharp knife, starting at his belly, like this."

"Why do you have to do that?" I asked.

"To scoop out his guts because you don't eat guts unless you've no money, and then you eat tripe."

"What's tripe?" I said.

"Tripe, my boy, is cow's stomach."

"Ugh! That's disgusting!" I exclaimed.

"Some people like it, and some people eat black pudding," he informed me.

"What's that? 'cos I love pudding," I asked, my interest revived.

"It's made from pig's blood. You see they hang the pig upside down and slit her throat and collect the blood. You can hear the pig screaming miles away."

"That's cruel," I cried out. "I'll tell the RSPCA." Unknown to my parents I had just been accepted as a very junior member, and had a certificate to prove it. I had written to say that if I saw a worm on the pavement I always picked it up and put it in someone's garden. Hilda's father knew I spent a great deal of time on farms, but while I spent those idyllic holidays on the farms of my uncles and aunts, all of whom were childless, I must have been inordinately spoilt and protected from anything distasteful. Sensing that, like his daughter, I was sickened by his talk, he made me a peace offering by handing me something he'd just taken from inside the fish. It looked like a tiny transparent sausage-shaped balloon.

"D'you know what that is?" he asked. I shook my head and must have looked nauseated because he then spoke more kindly.

"How d'you think a fish can swim at any level he wants to, under the water?"

"By wagging its tail and its fins."

"Yes, but to dive down he empties his swim bladder of air and to come up again he fills it with air; and that's a swim bladder you're holding in your hand."

I was so entranced, that when I got home I searched through a linen bag of offcuts and found a bit of purple velvet remnant, which I glued onto the outside of an empty matchbox. Then using thin white cotton, I tied the swim bladder onto the velvet-covered matchbox and fixed it inside a box of dates, which I first emptied by eating them all. The next week I took the whole item to school. Of course I showed it proudly to our troop on the way to school. But one of the girls went and told Guv Jones who called me out in assembly. I had to stand on a chair next to Guv Jones in front of the whole school.

She trumpeted, "This boy has a fish's bladder." Then she proclaimed, "He is the only pupil who has a fish's bladder ever to attend this school." I felt the chilling draught of air as, cloak whirling, arm extended, she suddenly turned towards me and boomed, "Now boy, tell us all about your bladder."

Some of the teachers and older children started tittering and soon the whole school was hooting with laughter, which stopped instantly as Guv Jones swung back to face the school, her sharp beaked nose cutting wide swathes through the air like a sword sweeping over our heads, while her black gimlet eyes beamed malevolence as she bellowed, "Silence!"

Exposed on a chair, like a freak exhibit at a fair, in front of the whole school and clutching my fish's bladder, I piped forth in a diminutive voice about fishes coming to the surface to catch flies, then diving down to eat them and how air went in and out of the swim bladder. That was my first public lecture and as a result I became the school naturalist. Children brought me all sorts of insects and creepy-crawlies to identify.

One day a bevy of big girls gave me a matchbox and when I opened it, a huge black hairy spider with a bloated body and thick bristly legs came out and ran up my arm inside my sleeve, and settled in my armpit. The girls screeched with joy as I ran wildly round the playground screaming and tearing my clothes off. I had to pick it out of my armpit. I can still hear the crack followed by the juicy squelch as I trod on it. Because of that horrible experience it is not surprising that I have become a lifelong sufferer from incurable arachnophobia. I hated those girls so much I might also have become a lifelong misogynist, were it not for Mary Leonard who ran over to me as I stood there alone in the corner of the school playground blubbering. She was not in my class and was a quiet, insignificant, sad-looking little girl with tangled mousy hair. She was always alone because none of the other girls would play with her. Hilda said it was because she was smelly and came from a slummy home, wore tatty cast-off clothes, was yukky and didn't speak properly; on top of that her father was a drunkard and her mother a slut who went out to work. All that prejudice evaporated when she came and stood by my side and put her arm around me.

"Don't you 'ave nuffink to do with them snobby girls. They're filffy rotten," she said as she consoled me.

I was grateful to her but even as I whimpered in a state of flesh-creeping shock and wretchedness, I couldn't help noticing the dried sleep in the corners of her tired eyes and the crusts of snot in her nostrils. There were scabs on her legs and her thin frock was torn and very skimpy. She stayed with me until the bell went and we separated to go back to our classes.

Sometime later, Hilda took great delight in telling me that she had overheard Guv Jones telling her mother that Mary Leonard had been stung on her bum by a bee when she sat down at her desk.

Hilda said, "Guv Jones had had to put iodine on the sting and was surprised that Mary Leonard's knickers were all shreds and tatters with big holes in them because she was so poor." I really loathed Hilda for that. In spite of the ragging I had to put up with from Hilda and David, I always stood up for Mary Leonard. She was kind.

There was, however, one girl in our school that David and I worshipped from afar. She was about Hilda's age and so must have been nearly eleven years old. Her long, shiny black hair came down to her waist and she was very, very pretty. Neither of us had ever dared to speak to her, but when we were out of breath from chasing and wrestling, we would become Hazel-watchers. One day when Hilda was not in school to shepherd us home, we followed Hazel at a distance to find out where she lived. For some unaccountable reason we congratulated one another that we had chosen a girl who lived in a nice big house like ours. David and I made a pact that when we grew up we were going to marry her.

A few weeks later David took me into a quiet corner of the playground and, plunging his hand into a pocket of his shorts, pulled out a small red box just like the boxes my mother kept her rings in. Making sure no one could see us, he handed me the box and said, "Go on, open it." It had a little spring in the lid and inside was a ring with sparkling blue and red stones.

"Crumbs! That's a beauty. Where d'you get it?" I said.

"From my sister's bedroom. She's got plenty."

"What d'you want it for?"

"Don't be so daft. If we're going to marry her, we've got to give her a ring so nobody else can marry her," he said with authority.

"That's great. We'll catch her after school."

We climbed up a tree by the school gates and hid there. We saw Hilda hanging around waiting for us, but eventually she made off leading her usual retinue of small girls. The last child to leave, slowly and alone, as though unwilling to go home, was Mary Leonard and David thumped me playfully in the ribs. Knowing that Guv Jones in her black cloak might swirl out of school

47

across the yard and sail though the gates at any time now, and that she would surely see us with her evil eye, we climbed down.

Hazel was not in school.

"What shall we do now?" I asked.

"Go to her house, stupid!" said David with the confidence born of one nearly a year older than me.

"OK, but what if her parents see us?"

"They won't," said David with conviction, as he juggled with the box in the pocket of his shorts, "We've got to give her this ring before somebody else gets her!"

On the way to her house we passed Mary Leonard trailing her way home.

"I seed you uffa tree. If you was waiting for 'azel 'orkins you've 'ad it, 'cos Miss said she's got 'erself very ill wiv a scarlet fever and vey're putting 'er in an 'orspital."

David ignored Mary Leonard but I thanked her and gave her one of my aniseed balls.

When I caught David up he said, "Why d'you talk to that horrid girl?"

"She's not horrid. She just told me Hazel has scarlet fever and they're taking her to hospital."

"That girl's potty and she tells stinking fibs and you're bats to talk to her."

With that I pushed him in the chest and he tumbled backwards over a low hedge onto somebody's front lawn. I jumped in on top of him and we wrestled our way all over the lawn and into some flower beds. It was then that an old man with a stick came out of his house.

"Gur ur uv it, you dirty little buggers! I'll tan your backsides 'til you can't sit down!"

We didn't wait for a second invitation but ran all the way to Hazel's house, just in time to see someone on a stretcher covered with a very red blanket being carried into an ambulance. It sped away down the road.

48

"P'rhaps that wasn't Hazel 'cos when I had scarlet fever I didn't have to go into hospital," I said hopefully.

"Well I dare you to go and ask!"

"No, you do, 'cos you've got the ring."

"You're a cowardy cowardy custard!" taunted David.

"No I'm not, you are!"

With that we started fighting again. We were rolling around on the pavement in front of Hazel's house when a lady came out and asked us very nicely why we were fighting. We must have felt a bit silly because I said, "Sorry," and David said, "It's only a friendly," whereupon the lady asked us what school we went to. Without thinking I told her, and David thumped me in the back, but the lady said, "It's all right, I won't tell Miss Jones."

"D'you know her?" I asked.

"Yes, my daughter Hazel goes to her school."

Seeing our faces become suddenly red she asked, "Are you the two boys Hazel said have been following her around?"

Caught off guard I blurted out, "Oh no! We're just on our way home from school."

"That's odd, because I've not seen you pass this way before."

Why he came out with it I don't know but David said, "We've got something for Hazel."

I could have clobbered him and Hazel's mother said, "How very kind of you. I'm going up to the hospital to see Hazel this evening, so I'll give it to her."

The effect was electric because all Mrs Hawkins saw was the rear view of two very muddy little schoolboys pelting down the road as though the old man with the stick was after them.

By the time Hazel came back to school a few months later David and I, unashamedly fickle, had been bewitched by Alice. Poor Hazel was just another girl who carried tales home to her mother. Oddly enough it all came about through Hilda, though if she had known what would happen as a result of her father's kind invitation to David and me, she would most surely have blocked it. Hilda's father was a governor of a school and he had asked us to a performance of *Alice in Wonderland* in the school grounds – Hilda did not come as she had already seen it. That glorious summer evening Hilda's father took us to the school in his car. As we were driven through an entrance with massive wrought iron gates on either side, a man standing there saluted. I knew Hilda's father better than David did because he used to take me fishing, and so it was me who chirped up, "Who's that?"

"That's the gatekeeper and he lives in that little house alongside the gates – it's called the west lodge."

"The gate in our school goes straight into the playground," I said. "Haven't the children in your school got a playground?"

"Oh yes, they've got hundreds of acres of playground."

Not to be left out of the conversation David asked, "What's an acre?"

"It's the size of a small field – about twice the size of your playground in school."

"Crumbs!" said David.

"Crikey Moses!" I said and we both fell silent in awe.

The drive wound upwards through rolling parkland with woods, shrubberies and grassy hollows for about half a mile until we reached the front of the school, which turned out to be a rambling old grey stone mansion guarded by ancient oak trees. Its long windows sparkling in the evening sunshine blinked enquiringly at us. Rows of chairs were arranged in semicircular fashion around the upper lawned terrace and most of the seats had already been taken. However, we were ushered to reserved front seats, and Hilda's father disappeared into the school. We had never been to an open-air theatre before. We crouched forward in our seats with our heads close together and spoke in whispers so no one could hear.

"Why can't we come to this school? There's great places to make dens and hide, and lots of trees to climb. They'd never find us," whispered David.

"When I get home I'm going to ask if I can come here – and you do the same," I said in a hushed voice.

"OK. This is much better than our school and I bet . . ."

A crabby old woman sitting behind us tapped David on the shoulder and said, "It's just going to start."

We looked up and saw the performance was in fact starting. A man was talking. He said he was going to read some poetry. David and I groaned as he droned on and on. When he finished everyone clapped and we thought it was because the audience was glad he'd finished and so we clapped too. Then this girl nobody had noticed was climbing down from a huge oak tree at the side of the house and the poetry-man said that her name was Alice and she was pretending to be falling down a rabbit-hole.

I whispered to David, "She's a good climber for a girl."

"Yep. Nice too!"

We spent the whole of that balmy evening with our eyes glued to the girl who didn't seem to be much older than us. We followed her every move as though we'd never seen a girl before. She had long fair hair and very blue eyes. She wasn't just pretty like Hazel was. She was really beautiful. She was wearing a wisp of a blue frock and I said in a hushed voice, "Why is the bottom of her frock in ribbons?"

"Dunno, but it's nice. I wish all girls wore ribbony frocks," he sighed.

51

The March Hare, the Mad Hatter and the Cheshire Cat left us cold, but Alice had become our princess.

On the way home Hilda's father asked if we had enjoyed ourselves and said, "Didn't the March Hare and the Queen of Hearts act well!"

"Oh yes, very well," but we were too shy to say anything about Alice, or to ask anything about her, because he was a grown-up and wouldn't understand.

Over the next few days David and I shared our dreams about Alice and a week or so later we wrote down some of them in a letter, which we both signed and hid under a heavy trunk in a shed in my garden. We decided to find out her real name and address and send her our letter.

Soon afterwards my parents and I had dinner with Hilda's parents and Hilda. As was usual Hilda and I were excused after the pudding to go and play. While we were lolling about behind the sofa, Hilda decided to show me some boring photographs taken during her family holiday in Greece. I brought the subject round to the play and asked what Alice's real name was, and where she lived.

"I'll ask Daddy though I don't suppose he'll know because there are millions of children in the school." Then she carried on boring me with her stupid photographs, until our mothers came into the drawing room and wanted to know what we were doing behind the sofa.

I told David that I'd tried to coax Hilda to ask her father about Alice and a few days later on the way to school he questioned her as well.

Feigning sudden surprise she said, "Golly! I completely forgot. Why d'you want to know anyway?"

"Oh, just for fun," said David, trying to be as nonchalant as a ten-year-old possibly can be.

"You're both blushing," yelled Hilda, and to the other girls, "Look at their faces."

"They've gone all red!" screamed a dopey girl with a face like a bowl of cold porridge.

"Oh shut up you soppy things!" I snapped.

Hilda must have told them because, though no one else in our school would have seen the play, they all started chirruping a monotonous chorus in their shrill voices, "He's in love with Alice! He's in love with Alice!" pointing alternately at me and then at David. We were outnumbered and had no alternative but to shout back at them. But they just stood there, the five of them, feet planted firmly on the pavement, arms akimbo, necks craned forward, mouths wide open like small birds in a nest, bobbing up and down in time with their idiotic sing-song chant. Eventually we took to our heels and hid behind a parked car. As they passed we leapt out at them, frightening them with our hooting and whooping and chased them up the road, until Hilda brought them to a halt because she had seen Blanec the bogeyman hiding in a doorway, but in reality because she was out of breath.

Unfortunately the whole school soon got to know about Alice, and David and I were teased mercilessly by the girls, but when the boys started taunting us it was different.

"What's she like then? 'Ave you kissed 'er?"

Then the school bully, a big, coarse, lumbering lout lurched over to David and shouted out, "'Ave you 'ad 'er then?"

David lunged up at him but was soon overpowered. I ran over from the other end of the yard to find poor David flat on his back with the bully kneeling astride him pummelling his face and chest. I jumped on his back and dragged him off and the three of us started wrestling, twisting and turning over and over on the tarmac. David and I had had plenty of practice wrestling with one another and between us soon had the bully on his back, the two of us astride him, while the dozens of children standing round us in a circle hooted with delight. I was used to riding horses so knew how to grip his chest firmly between my knees, but as I threw my arms up in the air as a sign of victory, he punched me hard in the face. Now David and I had always considered boxing a dirty cowardly game and I had never actually punched anyone, but this was different. This vulgar thug had insulted Alice. I punched him as hard as I could and David rolled off him and held his arms to enable me to continue to punish his snarling face.

Then David shouted, "Come on, let me have a go at his ugly mug."

But as we changed places he managed to throw some damaging punches at David's face. However, once I had pinned his arms down, David got astride him and used the bully's screwed up face as a punch ball. We were both incensed by what he had said and while he yelled, kicked and swore, we made as great an impression on him as our little fists were able, until he cried out 'Pax!' and crossed his fingers.

The end result was that I had to explain to my mother why my shirt was bloodstained and my nose swollen – I'd tripped in the yard and fallen on my nose which bled; whereas David had fallen onto a water pipe sticking up out of the ground and that accounted for his black eye. Our mothers didn't really believe us and our fathers merely grinned. The bully was absent from school for the rest of the week. When he returned David and I took care always to be within sight of one another in the school yard.

We noticed that boys who had been threatened or actually bullied, tended to stick close to us even when we went to the 'dubs'. We didn't entirely relish this attention because we were not 'gang' boys – we were 'best pals' and that was enough for us. However, we did make occasional exceptions and allowed certain boys to undergo our secret initiation rites, so long as they qualified by being able to pee high enough on the wall of the 'dubs'. Naturally no girls were allowed.

However, Fulvia Averbuck with the dark hair and eyes and pretty blonde Bathsheba (Babs) Robinson with her deep blue eyes had always been our faithful schoolyard friends. We often evaded Hilda to rendezvous with them when one of us – usually one of them – had sixpence to spend. The four of us would giggle our way to Mrs Biggs' tuck-shop which lay in the opposite direction from our way home, so we were safe from Hilda. It took us an exquisite eternity deciding between aniseed balls, gob stoppers, pear drops, mint balls, liquorice and sherbet, but fat Mrs Biggs was very patient waiting for her sixpence. One day, meandering homewards full of sweets we suddenly and quite surprisingly started talking about getting married – Fulvia and David and Babs and me, but they didn't think their parents would allow it because we were not Jewish, though at that time we were too young to comprehend. In any event we were blissfully unaware that there was any controversy concerning the question of miscegenation. We didn't really care anyway because we had Alice.

In spite of repeated requests Hilda refused to tell us anything about Alice. We plied her with her favourite sweets but to no avail.

"We'll never ever talk to you again unless you find out about Alice," we said.

She just replied, "You're a pair of silly asses!" and strutted away to marshal the cluster of young girls who always seemed to be eagerly awaiting her.

One day when Hilda's father took me fishing, I waited for Hilda to disappear before telling him how

55

much David and I had enjoyed the play. I said we both hoped there would be another performance, blatantly touting for an invitation, but nothing came of it. David and I then thought of waiting at the school gates to give her our letter, but we didn't know where the school was; all we knew was that it had taken a long time to get there by car, so it must be miles away, but anyway neither of us had a bike. We could think of nothing else we could do and so sadly we retrieved the letter we had written to the magic dream-girl we idolized. We sealed it in a fresh envelope which we wrapped in a piece of red velvet from my mother's bag of offcuts. We lined an Oxo tin with newspaper, placed our letter carefully inside, closed the lid tightly and secured it with a couple of yards of string. That autumn evening at dusk we carefully buried the Oxo tin in a far corner of my garden.

For some time we had toyed with the idea of organizing a museum in a shed we were allowed to use in my garden. But when we heard that they were building the largest liner in the world in Glasgow, our enthusiasm to build our own version of this liner completely took over. Grown-ups kept referring to it as 'she' though we couldn't understand how a ship could be a girl. We used the same name as the shipbuilders and called it the '534'. We were adapting it for use on land using our roller skates and we welcomed Ronnie as a helper, although he was a bit younger than us, because he had given us his old roller skates. He later borrowed a pair from his sister so the '534' would run on a grand total of thirty-two wheels.

The patio at the bottom of the drawing room steps became a shipyard littered with pieces of wood, wire coat-hangers, tangled string, various hammers, boxes of nails and small boys. It echoed to the continual tap-tap-

tapping of hammers on nails, interspersed with occasional loud impatient banging, which was invariably followed by the ugly sounds of splintering wood. When this happened the continuous chirruping of treble voices became a high pitched cacophony, as the unfortunate culprit was subjected to a shrill tongue-lashing.

An outcry would ensue, "You stupid idiot! Look what you've done."

Another would sing out in support, "Go and get your eyes tested."

The culprit would turn on his tormentors, "Shut up you jibbering idiots! Go and get your little brains tested!"

"No point in a silly ass like you going to get your brain tested, because you haven't got one!" was the obvious rejoinder, and so it went on until someone else transgressed when the verbal ding-dong would begin all over again. But on the whole we were an amicable team of shipbuilders.

It took us a few weeks to fashion a fairly large platform made of pieces of wood nailed and wired together. We made it large enough so that we could give rides to other children not fortunate enough to own a '534'. To fix the pairs of roller skates underneath the platform was a problem, but Ronnie persuaded his father, who had a drill, to make holes in the wood so that we could thread cord around the roller skates to tie in a knot on top of the platform. The fourth pair of roller skates we tied together and fixed loosely at the front end and, using bits of wood and string, devised a Heath Robinson contraption to steer the land-liner. After building up the sides to about a foot above platform level and painting '534' in large white figures on both sides, we fixed an old wooden trike seat for the driver.

We were ready for the off.

However, our parents forbade us to take '534' anywhere near the road, so we had to content ourselves with rides up and down the drive, because the small wheels sank into the lawns.

We had not invited Hilda to help us but soon after we had built '534' she appeared with two small girls in tow.

"What on earth is that ridiculous contraption?" she said.

"Haven't you heard of the '534' or have the three of you been too busy playing with your dolls?" we replied.

"You're just like toddlers giving each other little rides up and down this drive," she sneered.

"Oh no we're not! You don't even know what the '534' is, you stupid things!"

"Oh yes we do," said Hilda, "and I bet that botched-up thing would fall to bits if you took it on the road."

"We're not allowed to take it on the road."

"Well take it on the pavement, you clots!" she said. "The pavement goes downhill just like the road does, you idiots!"

David, Ronnie and I went into conference. We decided we would not be disobeying our parents if we launched '534' on the pavement, because anyway it wasn't the road.

"How much d'you bet us?" we asked.

"Three aniseed balls."

"Show us 'em."

"I'll get them in the tuck-shop after school on Monday," said Hilda.

"OK then! But you've got to come with us."

So it was that '534' was dragged outside onto the pavement and six children, whose ages ranged from 7 to 10½ years, boarded the land-liner at the top of a moderately steep hill. The pavement was bordered on one side by stone walls or hedges, and on the other side by a wide grass verge with fairly large ash trees every few yards. David and I being best pals agreed to steer together, both of us astride the wooden trike seat; David being older was in front while I was right up close behind him. We were tightly packed with Ronnie and Hilda sitting on the platform behind us while the two small girls were squeezed right up at the back, but they were quite safe because the platform had a back as well as sides.

This was the long-awaited day; the real launch of '534'.

"Anchors away!"

"Yippee!"

"Here we go"

"Whoopee!"

With shouts from us boys, number '534' began to move slowly down the hill. The roller skate wheels made regular clicking noises as they ran over the uneven joints between the granite paving slabs, and the various pieces of wood in our masterpiece began to move together in harmony. But as the platform gained speed, so we heard discordant noises, which increased in frequency and volume, until '534' became a veritable sounding board of loud, jangling, rasping dissonance and David and I were obliged to shout instructions to one another in order to be heard.

"Look out!" shouted David, "there's an old chap in the middle of the pavement with his back to us."

"He must be stupid or deaf!" I yelled back. "Hoi! Get out 'er the way!"

By now our land-liner was travelling at speed and the little girls were screaming, "Stop! Help!"

In our frantic attempts to avoid the old man we pulled on the right hand steering rope as much as we dare and just managed to miss him by inches. As the land-liner sped past him at a rate of knots all we heard was, "What the hell! You bloody fools!"

During this manoeuvre the right hand side of '534'

had brushed up against a hedge but we skilfully steered it back on course. The girls were still screaming, "Please stop! Please!" but we boys were whooping it up, hollering and hooting with the wind in our hair, as our very own brainchild went hurtling headlong down the hill gathering momentum. Nothing was further from our minds than a fact we'd overlooked. We had no brakes! We were speedway racing drivers making our attempt on the land speed record and no screaming girls were going to stop us.

But then one of them grabbed Hilda from behind and cried out in panic, "Hildy, stop them – pl-e-e-eze!" Hilda's response was immediate. She snatched at the left hand steering rope and jerked it so violently that our beloved '534' went careering into a tree. David and I were pitched forward into the tree, while those behind were propelled over our heads, landing in a heap on the grass verge. Both of the small girls, who had described the most spectacular arcs through the air, had cuts on their hands and knees and continued screaming. However, what concerned David, Ronnie and me was that our precious '534' was lying in pieces; it had been shattered by the force of the impact. But one piece of wood stood upright against the tree. It proudly proclaimed '534' in bold white figures. But it looked like a gravestone.

We rounded on Hilda, "You blithering idiot, look what you've done. You've wrecked '534'! Why did you have to do that you ruddy cretin!"

"You're three silly asses! You were going too fast. You nearly killed that old man."

"But we didn't. Why don't you go home and take your cry-babies with you!"

As the small girls ran off shrieking, followed by a rattled Hilda, the deaf old fool whose life we'd saved by our brilliant navigation came shuffling up, but it was obvious he had no intention of thanking us. His face was purple and his false teeth were floating around his mouth, chattering independently of his rapid lip movements. The only words that came spluttering through the froth in his mouth were, "Hooligans! Savages! Police," and all he saw through his thick spectacles were three pairs of heels.

Some hours later we went back to the wreck of our land-liner, retrieved our roller skates, the '534' name boards and some of the flotsam from around the tree. We hid the sad remnants of our dream-ship in the shed. We told our parents we had dismantled the land-liner because 'it didn't work properly' but we were keeping one of the name plates '534' as an exhibit for the museum we were soon going to open.

Our only satisfaction was to hear that Hilda had been thoroughly carpeted for her irresponsible behaviour when she was supposed to be in charge of the two small girls who, apart from cut hands and knees, we heard were 'covered in bruises'. She was never to be allowed to take them out or have anything to do with them again.

The real '534' was launched later than ours and was called 'Queen Mary', but years afterwards my father told me that the owners, Cunard, had wanted to name the ship 'Queen Victoria'. They had asked King George V for permission to name the ship after 'the greatest queen this country has ever known'. The King said, "That's a great compliment to my wife. I'll ask her," and of course she agreed!

After concealing the truth about '534', just like Cunard did, David and I, with a sudden gush of overflowing enthusiasm natural to small boys, set about our next grand project – the Museum. We were fortunate in that my parents at no time tried to dam back the eagerness that now welled up inside us, as we started clearing enough space in a shed in my garden to house the wonderful displays people would be queuing up to see. Next on the agenda was the quest to find interesting items to fill that space.

It was my caterpillar-period and I had a collection of various caterpillars all happily feeding on different sorts of leaves. They were housed in a special cage which Hilda's father had had constructed by the woodwork master in the school he governed and had given me as a birthday present. Hilda of course had pointed out at my birthday party that the woodwork master had been her father's batman in the army.

David brought an ostrich egg and a quiver and my friend Norrie lent me his brother's collection of birds' eggs, all neatly labelled, together with an almost complete set of cigarette cards of famous cricketers. From my own house I borrowed the yard-long, beak-like toothed upper jaws of two Japanese saw-fish, and added my two albums of foreign stamps and a small box of foreign coins from my bedroom. David's aunt who'd lived in India lent us the skin of a python twenty-eight feet long, which we draped around three sides of an exhibition area. Ronnie's father lent us a blowpipe which, according to him, the chief of a savage tribe in the jungles of Malaya had given him in exchange for a few coloured beads. We also had a dead hedgehog which we found in the garden and soaked in a bucket of boiling water to kill the fleas. Various other grown-ups who were friends of our parents lent us exhibits, ranging from semi-precious stones and fossils to a stuffed owl.

We labelled the exhibits in joined-up writing and made up sensational and bloodcurdling stories about some of them. One of the Japanese saw-fishes had sawn a man into two halves, and the other had sawn its way into the belly of a whale to try and rescue Jonah. The python had wrapped itself around a man and crushed him, bones and all, until he was the shape of a sausage and then swallowed him whole. The quiver was the one used by Robin Hood, and the blowpipe had been used to fire poisoned darts at two white missionaries who died in agony. We took a splinter from a bamboo stick in the garden and sharpened one end which we painted red – this was the actual dart that had killed one of the missionaries and that was his blood.

During the course of conversation my parents must have mentioned the museum to Hilda's parents because just before the Grand Opening, Hilda appeared with an armful of exhibits including the shrunken head of a boy from South America, a buffalo's horn and a honeycomb, so we had to let her in. She was obviously chastened as a result of her telling-off for the '534' incident, because she wasn't nearly as bossy, but she had to get her oar in and said to me rather condescendingly, "Oh, you're showing the caterpillar cage my father's batman made for you." She continued in a patronizing manner, "You've made quite a good job of this," and then with the mentality of someone in trade, "How much are you charging for admission?"

"Nothing. It's only for our friends."

"You should charge a penny for adults and a halfpenny for children and you should advertize it."

"OK, you do that then," we said hoping she would go away, but no such luck. She was determined to barge in and interfere with our plans.

"You should take the visitors around the museum – no more than two at a time – and know how to answer all their questions."

The next day some of our donors came to see the museum. Hilda had provided a cocoa tin with a slit in the top to collect the money. A friend of my mother's who had been a medical missionary in India came to the museum and told us that large pythons swallowed men who were still alive and kicking, so we added that gruesome detail to the label. Hilda, who noticed such things, told us the lady had put sixpence in the tin.

My mother was very surprised one day to find two strangers and a child, who had visited the museum, wandering around the house. They ordered 'cream teas', but were politely sent on their way. We found that Hilda had placed a board at the bottom of the drive advertising the museum:

MUSEUM TOUR – ONE PENNY
MUSEUM TOUR WITH CREAM TEA –
FOUR PENCE
CHILDREN HALF PRICE

This was the first intimation my parents had that visitors were being charged for entry to the museum. We were roundly reprimanded and told we would grow up to be commercial travellers if we carried on like that. The collecting tin was confiscated and we had to return the money. The board was removed and so was Hilda.

From then on the museum was patronised almost exclusively by small boys we managed to inveigle into the shed. We then proceeded to frighten them with blood-curdling yarns about the exhibits. Pointing to the python skin we would tell them how a man had been found still alive with all his bones crushed inside the belly of this python. They'd had to make three swipes with a sword before they'd managed to slice his head off and put him out of his agony, so that then they could hack him into small pieces to get him out. The South American boy had had his arms and legs broken because he'd been rude. He was in so much pain he screamed all night and because he'd kept the chief of the tribe awake, the chief gave the order that he was to be killed that morning. They couldn't find the axe and so they had to saw his head off using a rusty saw with jagged teeth and it took ages. That was why the boy looked so terrified and as though he were still in pain, with his mouth wide open and his eyes popping out of his head. We had found a broken rusty old saw in the woodshed and put some red paint on it and placed it next to the boy's head. Of course we said that it was the very one that had been used. They were told also that if they didn't behave they would be pricked with the poisonous dart that had killed one of the missionaries and they would be sure to die screaming and in terrible pain.

After two mothers complained that their children were having terrifying nightmares after visits to our shed, our parents summarily closed the museum. The exhibits were returned to their owners and David and I resumed our old way of life. We spent those long hot summer days building tree-houses and secret dens, wrestling and dreaming in the long grass of the buttercup field.

Years later the gardener unearthed the Oxo tin and gave it to my parents. It was my mother who was shocked at the thoughts that had gone through our minds when we were little boys. My father just laughed.

Rites de Passage?

Were our schooldays really all that happy? For me they are certainly a long time ago.

The move from a warm, brick-built primary school where boys and girls were happy being taught together by gentle lady teachers, to a cold, damp, ramshackle wooden hut in the grounds of a boys' public school with stern-faced men in swirling black gowns, caused much apprehension in us new boys. This was somewhat allayed by 'Tom Bott' an aptly nicknamed teacher of general subjects who, in spite of (or because of) whacking boys into shape with his stick Excalibur, is warmly remembered. Excalibur often disappeared and, until found or replaced, he would belabour us with the large knot he'd tied in his tattered gown, but without much effect because he couldn't get the necessary swing.

From swapping caterpillars in matchboxes and playing pop-alleys on the way home from primary school, to being the youngest, loneliest boy in a public school was a powerful psychological shock. Masters in Dracula-cloaks had to be obeyed, school uniform, including caps, had to be worn and friendly monitors were replaced by overgrown boys called prefects, who had authority to cane younger boys and so also had to be obeyed. Even worse, I was separated from my cousin David, my best pal since I was four years old, who didn't manage to get into my school and had to go to a boarding school which he hated.

Our headmaster, who wore a wing collar and carried a silver-headed walking stick, was a kind and dignified man who knew every boy in the school by name. It was indeed an unhappy day for the school when he left at the end of my first year. Many eyes were brimming as he shook hands and said a personal goodbye to each of us that sad, summer afternoon. He had abolished Saturday morning school and had made rugby the official winter game. Years later I learnt it was through his efforts that the school had become such a centre of excellence, that he had been invited to become one of the hundred and fifty members of the Headmasters' Conference of Great Britain. This in turn attracted the very best masters who incidentally, in my day, all knew and good-naturedly accepted their nicknames ranging from Bugs through Crippen, Dicky, Felix, Grunter, Junker, Soak to Spicey, the one exception being Boozy who beat boys he overheard using it. Some were scholarship boys but most of the entrants were fee-paying, having passed the entrance examination, while those who failed were sent to the local secondary school.

During that first year two masters with a couple of prefects as helpers, took the two lowest forms for a day trip to the recently opened Whipsnade Zoo. The only creature I recall is a seven-foot-tall emu, and that only because it took a dislike to a red-haired boy and bit his hand, drawing blood. One of my friends who had eaten an enormous amount of ice cream was sitting next to me on the bus journey back to Paddington. Not surprisingly he felt sick and the regular throb of the engine together with the irregular lurching of the bus didn't help. I remember being amazed at the sheer volume of red and green vomit that suddenly gushed out of his mouth through the open window. I ducked to avoid it as it blew back into the bus, but other boys, not so lucky, were bespattered. Now a smug pillar of society, he would not care to be reminded of this, any more than would those small boys who, one by one, were dragged protesting into our compartment on the train, to be 'operated upon' by one of the prefects who granted us, the uncomprehending onlookers, immunity so long as we held our tongues.

That trip came to a bloody end for as the train drew into the railway station, one excited boy in my compartment, seeing his father waiting on the platform, thrust his head through the window to greet him. Unfortunately the window was closed. Bleeding profusely he was rushed to the local hospital to be stitched up and, if he is still around, no doubt bears the two-inch oblique scar on his forehead as a permanent reminder of how clean train windows used to be.

When I was eleven years old, I broke my arm showing off on my bike and was caught telling a friend all about it during a maths lesson. The young master called me out and made me stand in front of the form. Talking in class was a punishable offence, but I reckoned that with my broken arm I would be immune from corporal punishment. To my disbelief, he asked in his affected voice, "Hes enyone heah a slippah, size ten pwefwebly?" Fortunately he only managed to get a size seven, but it still hurt. That day I learnt what 'adding insult to injury' meant.

A year later I learnt from another master that 'silence is golden'. On that occasion it was the master who suffered the injury and I suffered the insult. While showing us an experiment during a physics lesson he broke a piece of glass tubing and cut his fingers. He held them under the water tap and applied tincture of iodine which of course just ran off the wet skin. He overheard me telling the boy next to me that if he had any sense he would dry his fingers before putting the iodine on. Still bleeding he made me bend over and besides learning that 'silence is golden', I learnt that the stinging from knotted rubber tubing lasts longer and is more painful than that from any slipper.

Though one of my best friends, 'Jammer' Jackson,

had good cause to disagree with me the following term, as a result of what happened to him during a gym lesson taken by a stand-in master. We had been allocated partners to practise doing handstands. I had a small slim boy who was easy to handle, but poor Jammer had an extremely plump boy called 'Slobby' Smith, who was so clumsy that when he kicked his great tree-trunk legs up in a half-hearted way, Jammer was unable to hold them and they slithered out of his hands and the fat boy collapsed in a heap on the floor. He started wailing peevishly, "Sir! Sir! My arm hurts. Jackson let me fall, sir." Whereupon Jackson said, "Shut your mouth you great fat slob!"

Unfortunately the gym master overheard and said, "Come here boy, what's your name?"

"Jackson, sir."

"I will not have that sort of language in my class. Take one slipper off Jackson and bring it to me."

"Yes, sir," said Jammer taking it off and handing it to the master.

"I'll show you another use for a slipper."

Knowing what was coming it was unfortunate for Jammer that the regulation gym kit consisted of only small white shorts and white plimsolls – no vest, pants or socks were worn. Incidentally our name for plimsolls was 'daps' while the masters called them 'slippers'.

"Bend over that horse, Jackson."

"It's too high, sir."

"Don't argue, boy. Get right up across it, or d'you want me to help you?"

Poor Jammer hoisted himself up onto the horse and lay across it almost upended, feet off the floor. Placing the dap across the well-displayed, eminently accessible target area, the master made a few practice swipes without actually touching the shorts. While his victim, gripping the legs of the horse, waited quivering, the master took his time strolling to the far end of the gymnasium. Then suddenly turning, he sprang into the brisk run-up. The loud resounding thwack of the rubber sole through the thin cotton gym shorts onto Jammer's poor upturned bottom and his cry of pain, caused us all to take a sharp intake of breath as we cowered against the wall bars.

"You'll get an extra stroke each time you make a sound," the master said, and proceeded to repeat the whole process. Each time he brought the dap down with brute force onto Jammer's defenceless behind, I could almost feel the searing pain myself. Jammer was very brave and took his remaining seven cruel strokes without a murmur. He got down off the horse without a word, though his cheeks were wet. Not surprisingly, it was obvious in the showers afterwards that his punishment had been far worse than mine had been the term before. Over the next few days two of us lent Jammer our coats to sit on during lessons. Our proper gym master, Junker, came back to school the following week and must have wondered why he had such a welcoming class.

One afternoon after school later that term, when there were no prefects about, Jammer and I caught Slobby Smith and marched him to the far side of the playing fields and dragged him into a coppice out of earshot of the school. We told him we didn't like boys who squealed and he was going to be disciplined and given a taste of the punishment he'd made Jammer suffer. Knowing we were absolutely determined, he protested loudly and yelled and struggled so much we found it really hard work to deal with him. He was so very plump it would have been easier wrestling with a jellyfish. At last, between us, we managed to master him. It was like walloping a pair of bouncy pink balloons, and he set up an incredible hullabaloo with his hollering and trumpeting. Breathless after our exertions we let him get up. Clutching his fiery-red backside he fled as fast as a chastened fat boy can. No one lent him a coat.

But the lash of a master's tongue loaded with sarcasm, usually reserved for boys in the middle school, was far more effective than any corporal punishment, but I escaped that, or maybe just wasn't old enough to comprehend. In any event the reprimand that had the most telling effect on me was one I received for chalking silly slogans on the black walls of the dark room, when I was just fourteen years of age. It was delivered to me privately by Soak, the chemistry master, who merely asked me in a quiet yet authoritative voice, whether I didn't consider my action childish.

As schoolboys in a prestigious boys' school my generation was fortunate indeed to receive the very best education possible, enjoying all the advantages, without any of the disadvantages, of boarding schools. Indications are that single-sex education at that level still gives the best all-round results. Strict discipline was maintained but we were allowed to develop individually and avoid becoming stereotyped. Although it was a day school, vague, yet deep, friendships did occur between boys.

One of the most amusing episodes in my school life followed an announcement in assembly directing all boys of fifteen years of age and over, to proceed to the lecture theatre at 10 o'clock that morning – no explanation was forthcoming. After three missing boys had been found and herded in by the prefects, the doors of the lecture theatre were closed, and the headmaster, putting on his frightening death's-head look, commanded silence. Any boy caught whispering was immediately named to report to his study after school, and we all knew what that meant. At last the doors were flung open and a neat little man in plus fours bounced into the room. With two prefects guarding the door, the headmaster announced in his sepulchral voice, his thin blue lips barely moving, that we were now of an age when, as part of our education, we were to be informed about – and he spat the word out in disgust – sex.

The effect was instantaneous. The tiers of bored boys sat bolt upright, leant forward expectantly, eyes glistening, as the little man prancing around the room told us in jocular fashion all he thought we needed to know about girls, while the headmaster looked as though he'd smelt a polecat.

Suddenly the mood changed. The little chap stopped jigging around, lowered his voice and, in conspiratorial tones, started telling us about boys. When he got to the bit about avoiding wet dreams by tying a hairbrush, bristles inwards, tightly around one's waist to prevent one lying on one's back, we couldn't wait to experiment. But it was when he said in measured tones, "One drop of this precious fluid is equal to sixty drops of blood," that one of the prefects guarding the doors turned pale green and left the room. A large boy in the back row slumped forward in a dead faint, and was carried out with difficulty down between the tiered rows by six very willing, pale-faced volunteers. It was some time before we found out that the plus-foured little joker had been talking nonsense, and far from being 'educated', I wondered just how much damage had been done that morning.

Some of the sixth-form masters were wise enough not to attempt to stifle the burgeoning idealism common to sensitive impressionable boys in their mid-teens. This was evidenced by their sympathetic treatment of two boys who declined to accept prefect badges because they considered the method of selection to be undemocratic. One sixth-form boy, so moved by Churchill's oratory

73

and reports of Nazi atrocities, protested, when an attempt was made to force him to take German as a subject, by goose-stepping in jack boots and riding breeches into the German class. In spite of threats from the headmaster, the attempt was eventually abandoned and, as came to light years later, this was due to representations from a coterie of senior masters including the German master!

It was considered a mark of favour if one were asked to read the lesson in morning assembly. Strict adherence to the list of prescribed daily readings from the Gospels had been enforced since an episode many years previously when a boy, unaware of the list, chose his own reading from the book of Isaiah. As usual the reading failed to arouse the boys from their morning torpor, but when he came to the end, and in a clear voice read out with relish the four-letter words in the last verse, the effect was reputed to have been electric. Boys woke up, masters started forward, and it was said the headmaster made as if to savage the lad but he was too late – the boy was already saying, "Here endeth the lesson." It was rumoured that the boy was severely chastised.

Knowing that we were beyond punishment some of us, on the morning of our very last day at school, met at the taxi rank outside the railway station. We were wearing clothes borrowed from our fathers' wardrobes. We attempted to hire a taxi each to drive us to school, but only three taxi-drivers were sporting enough to agree. The rest took exception to the appearance of sixteen- and seventeen-year-olds carrying walking sticks and riding crops and dressed in an irregular assortment of bowler hats, tailcoats, jodhpurs, striped trousers, top hats and bow ties. One of them said, "It's more than my job's worth," while another reminded us there was a war on and a taste of army discipline was what we needed. A third said he was going to report us, which he must have done, because as we rolled up the drive we saw a posse of masters drawn up at the main doors of the school. Our drivers, entering into the spirit of the occasion, sprang out and saluted as they held the taxi doors open for us. Summoning as much dignity as schoolboys can, we strolled nonchalantly past the muttering masters into the main hall. There the whole school stood waiting for us, in order that assembly could begin with the reading of the lesson. As I was destined to do this, I was obliged to remain standing facing the boys who, together with some of the younger masters, were smirking as I placed my gloves, bowler hat and riding crop on a nearby table. Meanwhile the headmaster was fuming and frothing on the platform as he referred to the disgraceful behaviour that morning. I waited until he'd finished. Then I slowly and deliberately mounted the steps to the dais, fingering my jewelled cravat-pin and, standing at the lectern, polished and adjusted my monocle before I started to read in an ecclesiastical voice. While I intoned the final words, "Here endeth the lesson", I turned, clicked my heels and nodded to the universally disliked headmaster. As I bowed out and left the stage the applause was quelled on the instant by the ominously threatening contortions of the headmaster's face. At the best of times it was a grey mask drawn tight across a monkey-like skull, which swivelled unpredictably on top of a tall thin skeleton of a body. That morning it was even more frightening, as he ordered the miscreants to report forthwith to his study. The order was ignored.

Pupils who came to the school after Germany was crushed in 1945 could not share our memories of the lower school, our sticky visits to the tuck-shop and our furtive visits to the place where we could get real stink bombs for use at Speech Days. Nor could they share our memories of the silver barrage balloon, that giant monster tethered on the lowest grassy terrace, and its unpredictable antics when released in a high wind. Its cables brought down more chimneys than Messerschmitts, as the wailing air-raid sirens beckoned us, complete with gas masks, to the flooded air-raid shelters in the field adjacent to the playing fields. Saturday mornings were spent in the basement of the Kardomah café, now no more, where one cup of coffee bought us sixth-formers a few hours to play on the chess-tables and to shape our destinies. The two German cannons that stood in the school grounds, symbols of Germany's defeat in 1918, provided us with ample means of playing soldiers in our first year, but in our last year it was for real, and we were in at the birth of the Air Training Corps, which eventually grew into a top-flight squadron.

If only there had been camcorders then, to help recapture those moments of glory defending the name of the school in the mud of the rugby field, to help sense the keenness of inter-house competitions, and to rekindle the fiery schoolboy oratory in the Literary and Debating Society. Only too well do I still remember a fifteen-year-old boy blatantly using a swear word in the presence of a number of masters, knowing he would not be punished. The motion was, 'Science contributes more to civilization than Art'. Though a science pupil he declaimed with throbbing pulses and schoolboy fervour, "Armageddon's bloody dawn itself will be the work of science and of scientists." Had I known then what I know now, I would have said 'politics and politicians' instead of 'science and scientists'.

The exceptionally high teaching standard was matched by the dedication of masters who gave of their free time to infuse us with their enthusiasm. They ran clubs and societies for us, both on and off the playing fields. They made our school pre-eminent.

It is melancholy to record that the school has been demolished. But time weaves a rich pattern of multicoloured memories of schooldays, and of the school that gave so much and did its best to inspire the pupils to live up to its motto – our private guiding inspiration.

In the words of one of the last headmasters of the school, "Despite the demise of the school itself its traditions and ethos are alive and well, and will last until the final remaining former pupil of the school goes to meet the greatest headmaster of all."

ROWING

Before I learnt how to swim I was rescued from drowning on the last day of the holiday. Teifion and I were both eleven years old and were best friends. We had often been mistaken for brothers as we were both very fair, but in fact neither of us had any brothers or sisters – maybe that's why we were drawn so naturally to one another. That sunny September afternoon we had got tired of rowing around the harbour in a rubber dinghy we had borrowed from another boy, in exchange for our kite, and had started messing around in the warm sea near the lifeboat house. Romping about with the water just lapping our belly-buttons we were expending a vast amount of energy flailing our spindly arms and legs around, beating the placid sea water into flashing cascades of sunlight as we chased one another in our vigorous water-fighting.

Suddenly holding up my right hand with the first two fingers crossed in the then schoolboy code I cried "Pax!" whereupon Teifion immediately sang out in his treble voice, "OK, then let's go and sunbathe." At our age we carried out any change of plan immediately; so, pink and breathless, we darted out of the water and lowered ourselves gingerly face downwards onto the hot concrete, having decided, again instantly, that our bodies looked rather like uncooked chips and would look tougher with a fisherman's tan.

Within a few minutes I got bored with sunbathing and leaving Teifion stretched out dozing in his red trunks, I made my way to the wooden lifeboat slipway which was nearly all under water, the tide being in. It was easy walking down this warm, gently-sloping ramp into the sea. The water had covered the top of my trunks and was just up to my lower ribs when I began to slide down a slippery part of the slipway, and flapping my arms around trying to keep my balance only made me slip further and further down the ramp. Down I went floundering out of my depth, the water closing over my head. Thrashing around with arms and legs carried me beyond the end of the slipway into deep water; gulping sea water I tried to shout but only bubbles came out of my mouth. Brilliant yellow spots of light flashed around my head and I heard a piercing scream. My eyeballs began to burst and, surfacing, I glimpsed Teifion running and screaming, but I knew he couldn't swim either. My mouth, nose and throat were full of salt water. I was terrified, unable to breathe. Conscious of my heart pounding against my ribs, I sank, fighting against the pain in my chest as my ears burst in the all-pervading blackness.

I heard a treble voice, "Will he be all right?"

"Yup, but it was a damn' good job I was in the lifeboat house and heard you hollering, or he'd have been a gonner! Stupid little bugger! Is he your brother?"

"No, my pal."

"Well if I catch either of you kids arsing around this slipway again, you'll feel the weight of my 'and."

I was lying face-down being sick on the concrete, and Teifion was standing next to a big man in yellow oilskins.

"Soon as he's finished bringing 'is guts up, you can both bugger off."

With that the lifeboat man disappeared into the lifeboat house where he must have been working. When I stopped heaving, Teifion told me he'd heard a sort of throaty, gurgling noise, and seeing I was no longer lying alongside him realized the noises and the bubbles coming up out of the water were from me, and knowing I couldn't swim, had started yelling for help and pointing.

"Then that big chap in yellow dashed into the water up to his armpits, carried you out and dumped you here and you started puking."

"Crikey Moses! I feel lousy" was all I managed to say before I started shivering and heaving again. I tried to get up but slumped back down.

"I'm going to get someone to help," said Teifion, making as if to go to the beach, just a few hundred yards away beyond the breakwater.

"No, please don't," I said. "Don't leave me alone!" What I really meant was, don't go and fetch people here who'll go and tell my parents what's happened. Teifion stayed and I still remember his kindness and concern. He helped me sit up and dry using his own towel – I didn't have one, because the strict rule was that I was only allowed to go near the water if one of my parents was on the beach. He helped me dress before he dried and dressed himself. Even after all the years between, I still remember how, though normally we ran everywhere together, he walked slowly with me, and though we always had an ice cream and pop on the way up from the beach, he did not suggest it, no doubt knowing I would be sick, as indeed I was later. When we reached my gate I said, "Abyssinia."

"Abyssinia," sang out Teifion as he ran up the lane.

I never saw him again.

When I got in, my mother took one look at me and said I looked pale and ill, and asked what was the dried froth on my shirt and shorts.

"The man put too much ice cream into the cone and it spilt onto my clothes," I lied. "I've got a bit of a headache and I'm going to lie down."

Next day we left for home.

Years and years later, visiting old haunts, I enquired after Teifion. He is still remembered in New Quay as the kind and gentle golden-haired boy who was my pal. He had joined the Navy, and twenty years or so after he had saved me from drowning, he was buried at sea. I would not be writing this but for him. I never thanked him. But at that age one doesn't.

★　★　★

In spite of my near-death-by-drowning experience, my horror of mountains certainly does not extend to water, as was evidenced a year or so later when my school pal John and I were on holiday with our parents in Weymouth. We had left them on the beach and, unknown to them, had hired a rubber dinghy which we paddled straight out to sea. Whether or not it was our intention to land in France I do not know, but I have often wondered why, as I recall it, we were trying out our schoolboy French as we paddled away excitedly. Neither of us had a watch, but we must have been paddling for close on an hour and had failed to notice that there were no other rubber dinghies around – just a few yachts. We could see the people on the nearest yacht waving to us, and we waved back. They kept on waving and I said, "Les people sur la bateau-là sont jolly friendly. Peut-être nous sont know them."

"Il y a du people que mon père knows qui avez un bateau, which, by the way is masculine, avec la nom 'Lazy Days', mais je ne pas see la nom."

"Je ne pas vu le nom either mais ils seem être people très joli, and, tit-for-tat, 'nom' is masculine!" I retorted.

Our strokes had become slower and more laboured and I was beginning to feel chilly because we only had swimming trunks on, but of course I didn't admit that I felt cold. The gentle breeze had become more pronounced and the smooth surface of the sea had begun to ripple, and soon there were little choppy waves which started to rock our dinghy and make paddling together in time more difficult.

At last John said, "You cold?"

"Oui j'ai froid."

"Oh stop this stupid French stuff!"

"OK," I said gratefully.

With that we heard the rapidly increasing roar of a powerful motorboat bearing down on us. "Crumbs! Look out! Those idiots are going to run us down!" I shouted. With that it drew alongside. It was the coastguard with two red-faced angry-looking men aboard – our fathers!

There was quite a reception committee, some with binoculars, awaiting us when we reached shore and we felt like heroes – that is until our respective mothers started on us!

*   *   *

By the time I became friendly with Bill and 'Yank' in New Quay I had just reached the age of fourteen – he was called 'Yank' because his brother had been born in America and to us that was a good enough reason. We used to preordain each day as a day of 'blood-and-thunder' when we would try to raise Cain, or as a day of 'love-and-glory' when we would try to act agreeably.

We had just enjoyed a blood-and-thunder day – during which we tried, quite dangerously, to break one another's speed records by riding the iron trucks on the rails in the partially disused quarry – by making wailing ghost noises in the reputedly haunted and supposedly empty Memorial Hall to annoy and, we hoped, frighten the caretaker who was cleaning there, by scrumping apples in broad daylight and by collecting empty beer bottles from crates behind public houses and leaving a few dozen of them at night, prominently displayed, outside the main gates of the various manses and the vicarage and, baying loudly, again at night, outside the houses of people we did not like.

The next day was a love-and-glory day and Bill, who was a little older than us and who had to go somewhere with his parents that afternoon, had arranged for Yank and myself to meet two girls, who took one look at us, told us we were rather young and, suddenly remembering they had pressing engagements, scuttled off. Disappointed that we had failed to come up to expectations we did what we were hoping to have persuaded the girls to do – we went swimming in the sea. We swam vigorously for a whole hour, and followed this with a three-mile run along the beach, presumably to get fit and more macho, but in reality these were merely energy-sapping courses of action. Despite that, we then decided to go rowing, not to row sedately around the harbour like everyone else did, but to row out of the harbour beyond the end of the Pier, around the Headland and Carreg Walltog to the open sea and westward to Bird Rock and Carreg Draenog. Though yachts would sometimes round the Headland on that course we had never seen a rowing boat do so – so we had to!

After gulfing some greasy chips wrapped in newspaper, we commandeered a small rowing boat but did not mention our intention to anyone. We left a clutch of captive fathers rowing their excited, piping offspring in circles round and round the harbour, and after rounding the Headland we rowed westward, keeping well away from the jagged rocks under the cliffs. We took it in turns to row for about ten minutes each, though neither of us had a watch. It was fairly easy going and we reached Bird Rock in well under an hour. After messing about in the coves for quite a long time and generally annoying some of the thousands of birds on the Rock we started rowing back. It was my turn to row and I was surprised and a little hurt when Yank said, "Put your back into it. We've hardly moved in the last five minutes," because I was pulling as hard as I could on the oars, and wasn't particularly tired.

"Don't be such a moaner," I said. "You jolly well keep both your eyes open, 'cos it'll be your stupid fault if we crash into the rocks, you clot!"

"I'm doing my job. You do yours and pull harder, bird-brain!"

I thought this exchange was quite uncalled-for, being a complete reversal of the amicable relationship we'd enjoyed on the way out to Bird Rock, but I was not going to be outdone.

"Oh shut up you daft bat!"

And so it went on, but I soon realized it was only good-natured banter, though I also realized that our progress was in fact very slow. At the end of about ten minutes we changed places, a little nervously I thought; the sun had gone in behind a huge cloud and the water seemed darker and somewhat sinister, the cliffs black and forbidding, and it soon became apparent we were making barely any headway. The previously mill-pond surface of the sea seemed to be undulating in a gentle but persistent swell, and for the first time I wondered how deep the water was. At least I could swim a hundred yards now, but what good was that when the cliffs above us plunged vertically into the sea? Perhaps I could float until help came, but of course we had told no one where we were going. Yank had fallen uncharacteristically silent, and I wondered whether similar frightening thoughts were running through his mind. In any event our progress remained very slow but I made no comment because it was obvious he was really exerting himself.

Towards the end of my next spell with the oars, I noticed that I was grunting involuntarily with each stroke, and I was greatly relieved when Yank took over. By this time each of us, when rowing, was too breathless to say anything and the non-rower only spoke when it was necessary to give instructions to pull more strongly on one oar or the other. There were no other craft in sight, and though I was not alone, I began to feel lonely. The sea had now become distinctly unfriendly, heaving and swirling with suction from the deeps, the sky had clouded over and the cliffs had become quite malevolent. I countered these feelings by imagining I was riding a wonderful horse over gently undulating green meadows towards a delectable goal I was just about to reach, when I heard a testy voice, "Why don't you look where we're going, you idiot?" and I opened my eyes to the present just before I took over the oars. As the afternoon wore on and progress seemed to be getting slower and slower, each stint of rowing became more and more strenuous and the occasional provocative taunts lessened in frequency and intensity, probably because we realized we were now both fighting a common enemy, punching a punishing tide-flow.

At long last we rounded Carreg Walltog and the Headland hove in sight; only about three-quarters of a mile to row now. Involuntarily I gave voice, "Ahoy!" but the voice was parched and cracked.

But worse was in store for us.

The sea swell became more evident, and the fore and aft movement of our little boat became more pronounced. By now we were really fatigued and in an attempt to stave off complete exhaustion we both squeezed onto the thwart and took an oar each, but though the thrust-power driving the boat forward should have doubled, progress remained painfully slow – literally as well, for the front of my chest and shoulders were aching and each stroke aggravated my acute discomfort. Though it seemed uncharitable, I confess I was glad to see the agonized expression on Yank's face, lips drawn back with teeth bared, showing that he too was in trouble, and I ventured to suggest we rested on our oars for a little while. He readily agreed and we put our heads down between our knees. However when we sat up, we found that we had been carried back so far that we could no longer see the Headland. We later learnt that this was because of the strength of the tidal flow at mid-ebb spring tide, aided by a fairly strong east-north-east wind. We also found out later that it was these elements that had conspired to make our return from Bird Rock to New Quay Headland so very difficult, combined of course with the fact that our vigorous exertions, swimming and running, immediately prior to our rowing had sapped our energy.

We were now in dire straits, exhausted and being carried back too close to the rocks for comfort. After croaking a few curses at me for having suggested a rest we took up the oars again and, summoning all our remaining strength, we rowed painfully into the eye of the wind and against a spring tide, which we later learnt had been at mid-ebb, and therefore running at its strongest, at three knots or more, against us. The surface of the sea was heaving and a hostile wind was already whipping up and unfurling the crests of the small but burgeoning waves, forming frothy white seahorses. We were shipping large volumes of water with no means of baling it out, and were soaking wet and very cold. After what seemed an interminable purgatory of pain, the Headland and then the Pier came into view. We were utterly exhausted and were completely unable to respond to the hooting and jeering of the boys who had spotted us from the end of the Pier; their fathers were local fishermen who must have warned them of the crass stupidity of starting to row westward when a spring tide was beginning to ebb, unless of course one didn't plan on returning until the tide came back in, and ran with one, many hours later, making the return row easy.

However, when they saw our pitiful state their demeanour changed to one of solicitude and helpfulness. Later that evening, on top of the persistent ache in my limbs and chest, I suffered a sudden onset of quite severe difficulty in getting my breath and this frightened me. It was treated by the application of a most potent counterirritant – in my case the strongest and most concentrated alcoholic solution of iodine. The whole of the back and front of my chest was painted with this, so that I looked like a badly sunburnt Red Indian. I was put to bed propped up in a sitting position to ease my breathing, and was said to have an attack of "pleurodynia due to overuse and physical stress associated with dampness and cold" – and how!

Hearing of my plight, being confined to my bedroom, Bill came to see me, and I wondered why Yank hadn't called, until I learned that he too had had the strongest iodine treatment. Hardly a fitting end to a love-and-glory day for either of us!

The next time the three of us met, Bill was keen to have a love-and-glory day's rowing, but found that Yank and myself firmly rejected the proposal in favour of a quiet, terrestrial blood-and-thunder day, which, though a contradiction in terms, would be mere child's play compared with our love-and-glory day's rowing. This was the first and last time the three of us did not agree.

Bill became a Squadron Leader in the RAF and was killed in action. His name is on the War Memorial. Yank became an outstanding musician and died at the Salzburg Music Festival.

★   ★   ★

We were four lusty medical students about to enter our sixth and, we hoped, final year of study for the degrees of our various universities – Cambridge, London and Oxford – and one of us, Luke, prided himself in knowing something about sailing. Consequently he was deputed to do all the donkeywork of booking a yacht for a week's sailing on the Norfolk Broads that glorious summer long ago. Luke, who was the only one of us who held a driving licence, also persuaded his father to lend him an old car in which we left our renowned London teaching hospital and the sticky city with its tacky outskirts, and in a hundred and twenty miles or so, we arrived at a boatyard in Wroxham on the River Bure in the beautiful county of Norfolk. Soon after getting out of the car, we all spontaneously remarked upon the freshness and clarity of the air, which made us realize how polluted was the air we breathed every day in London.

And there she was waiting for us – *Sabrina*, trim, attractive with perfect form – inviting us four full-blooded males to board her, which with the impetuousness of youth we did. She was gaff-rigged, length overall 29 feet, and had a fore cabin containing two berths and a washbasin, and a saloon cabin which had two berths and a table. The cabins were separated by a companionway and WC compartment, and there were gas rings and an oven in the well. Brian and I immediately bagged the fore cabin leaving Luke and Dick to sort out the less private saloon cabin. There was also a rowing dinghy in tow. By mutual consent Luke was our skipper, who, though red-haired, was a level-headed, friendly sensible boy, but he was forced to treat his crew of three as numbskulled galley slaves, because we questioned his every command, largely because we were quite unacquainted with the lingo. "Do some quanting, you fools!" We did not realize that quanting was merely punting and we knew how to punt; though some years later, punting on the River Cam, I was too slow in bringing my punt pole down going under a bridge, and had it snatched out of my hands by some undergraduates standing on the bridge; they extracted a promise from me to treat them kindly in a viva exam the next day, before they gave it back – much to the amusement of the girl in my punt.

When Luke warned us not to wet the sheets, we told him not to be so rude, until we learnt that sheets were not sheets, nor even sails. But when it came to attaching the hanks to the forestay and rigging the jibsheets through the fairheads or cleating the halyards and fitting the boom to the gooseneck we, as mere crew members, were obliged to admit we knew nothing at all about sailing, and that Luke's commands were not pretentiousness on his part but necessitated his use of jargon; in fact within a few days we three crew members were using it ourselves but, like all amateurs, in a loud and ostentatious manner.

With a good wind it was great fun running on the starboard gybe and suddenly shouting 'ready about' (or was it 'steady about' – I can't remember), and seeing anyone stupid enough to be standing in the well at that time having to duck double-quick to avoid being clobbered by the heavy boom as one 'went about' to run on the port gybe.

When we became adept at handling *Sabrina*, it gave us great delight and a feeling of tremendous exhilaration, to sail across a wide Broad at a spanking pace, having harnessed a strong, fresh wind. On the other hand, to sail silently and gently in slow serenity, in that unique landscape of intertwined lakes, rivers, marshlands and windmills, was an experience to be treasured.

In the same way that horses and riders take precedence over other road traffic, so sail takes precedence over other craft and we derived great satisfaction going out of our way to force the fat old philistines, speeding along in their flashy motorboats, to give way to our beautiful yacht. We considered they were polluting and disturbing the peace of the lovely wetlands with their smelly, noisy engines and their blaring radios. After all, we reasoned, what would our greatest Admiral, Lord Nelson, who was born here and learned to sail on these very Norfolk Broads, think of them!

As the only smoker on board I generally had a late night pipe on deck before turning in, as the others objected to the smell of tobacco smoke in the cabins. It was then, alone, and moored on a quiet Broad, one could appreciate the timeless peace of those magic wetlands under a vast star-studded sky, with the moonlight dappling the water. One could listen to the silence, and know that time was immaterial in this precious silver landscape.

Brian and I being blond and fair-skinned kept our shirts on in the scorching sun, but Dick who had black hair but should have known better, stripped to the waist, and so occasionally did Luke. The result was that within two or three days both of them were suffering from quite severe sunburn with tender, lobster-red, blistered backs. Brian and I treated them by pouring cold water over them, and when they had dried we smeared a tinful of condensed milk over each back, because of course we had nothing fancy like sunburn lotion. The treatment didn't help, but Brian and I made the most of the situation, for when any chore needed doing, we only had to raise a hand as though to slap them on the back, 'come on old chap, cook us a decent meal' or 'the well needs cleaning', and the chore was carried out expeditiously, though not with too good grace. Brian and I prepared no meals, did no cleaning nor washing up for a few days, and any crockery that fell overboard into the mud was retrieved by the sunburnt pair we dubbed the 'Sundance Kids'. However, we were storing up a quiet resentment against ourselves, as we were soon to discover.

On our last afternoon we slipped a mudweight to the bottom on the River Bure near the village of Horning, and the four of us repaired to the Ferry Boat Inn nearby. It was fairly quiet and after a few beers Brian and I got bored, until we espied two girls at a table on the patio. In their late teens wearing skimpy dresses they too looked bored, so we joined them, leaving Luke and Dick nursing their sunburn with more beer. Both girls had just left school and were wondering what to do next, and being authorities on nurses at our teaching hospital, we considered ourselves admirably placed to offer them advice. They were on soft drinks, and since neither of us was a heavy-drinking rugby type, we joined them. It was almost as though a form of natural selection was at work, for as the lazy afternoon wore on, Brian confined his attentions to the tanned athletic blonde while the slim, pale, auburn-haired girl and I became closer. We wanted to take them on *Sabrina* for a gentle sail on Cockshoot Broad, less than half a mile down river, but the idea was resolutely opposed by Luke and especially by Dick.

This may have been as a direct result of what happened a month or so previously, when Dick and I, rowing on the river near Kingston upon Thames, had struck up a bargain with two attractive girls who were swimming, that we exchanged our boat for their bikini bottoms. But after our swim they kept us waiting in their tiny, tight bikinis for over an hour, wet and shivering on a small island in the river, before they returned in our boat with our clothes and their one towel, which was wet anyway because they had used it to dry themselves.

Since that episode Dick had become absolutely adamant that girls and boats were mutually incompatible, and so we acceded to the girls' suggestion to catch a bus and to go to the pictures in Norwich where they lived. Reminiscing many years later, neither Brian nor I could remember the name of the cinema, and certainly couldn't recall what was on the screen because we hardly saw it, our attention being directed elsewhere. But those girls – those lovely girls – we could hardly forget. Eventually, after spending aeons saying goodnight, we found the last bus had left hours ago, so we began our seven-mile walk back to *Sabrina*. There was no moon and the few cars that passed did not stop to give us a lift. When we arrived at the Ferry Boat Inn it was past 1 a.m., but *Sabrina* was nowhere to be found. The only sign that she had ever been moored there was the tiny little rowing dinghy.

"I just don't believe it," said Brian, "and not even a note!"

"It's the green-eye," I said.

"They'll be showing a touch of the yellow-eye when we find them."

"Well anyway which way are we going to row?"

"I'd say up-river because that's the way we were heading."

"OK," I said, "quarter of an hour each with the oars, there's no rudder and there's only room for one on that thwart so the one in the stern steers by mouth."

"'Steers by mouth', don't be so stupid!" said Brian.

"Don't you be so obtuse, you anog! Come on, I'll row first."

With that we untied the dinghy from its mooring and stepped into the little boat cautiously in order to avoid capsizing it and began rowing. Brian's voice rang out in a peremptory manner, "More to the right, more to the right, or we'll be in the bank."

"D'you mean my right or yours?"

"Mine of course, you clot!" he said, gesturing with his hand.

"That's my left you moron! Why don't you use the boat as reference like everyone else does and say 'starboard', you dumb cluck?"

"Aye, aye, Horatio."

Changing places was a perilous procedure since it was very dark, the dinghy was tiny and we were both six foot tall. Added to that, the mist which was rolling over the wetlands was becoming denser and denser, and we found it increasingly difficult to make out where the bank was, and when we ploughed into the reeds and mud of the marshlands an inevitable torrent of inane badinage followed. Eventually it became almost impossible to tell where the bank was, and one was forced to use an oar like an antenna to feel one's way. This delayed us even more, and the oar kept jumping out of its rowlock.

We had been rowing for over three hours. We were fatigued. We were very angry, and even more so when the mist started to lift very slightly revealing that we had just needlessly rowed all the way around the perimeter of Salhouse Broad, a distance of about one mile, and were re-entering the River Bure again exactly where we left it about three quarters of an hour previously; this was the result of following the bank in the dense mist, but what else could we have done? We had already decided on an appropriate punishment for our two yachting companions for leaving us stranded ashore with only a tiny dinghy. We drew a comparison with Captain Bligh and *The Mutiny on the Bounty*, conveniently overlooking the fact that the captain was still aboard, and that we were mere crew members adrift in a dinghy, but they had it coming to them. We were going to drag them out of their cosy cabin berths and throw them into the river; it would do their sunburn good too! Three quarters of an hour's arduous rowing later and the outline of a yacht came into view through the mist.

We approached silently and – Eureka! – There, with the aid of our small torch, was the yacht with the dinghy missing and the name 'Sabrina' clear on the stern. Soundlessly we hitched the painter to the stern, boarded and burst into the saloon cabin, grabbed one each, manhandled them struggling and screaming onto the deck but realized simultaneously we had a firm hold of two girls! "Bloody hell, let's get out of here," I said as we leapt into the dinghy, unhitched and rowed away like fury. Lamps were lit but too late to see us, men shouted but too late to find us, as we disappeared into the mist. Twenty minutes later we found our *Sabrina* and, much chastened, quietly boarded and crept guiltily into our berths. We agreed to say nothing to our two yachting companions and next day we left for London. Later we discovered that a number of yachts were named *Sabrina*, and each was designated by a number – a detail we had overlooked.

Three of us are still around. Brian has sailed away into the mists that await us all.

TO WALK WITH A CORPSE

The whispered mumbling sounds escaping from the slightly opened mouth, set under a pinched nose in a sallow cadaverous face, lent a somewhat sinister aspect to the large gangling frame of an acquaintance who had just come up to join me as a medical student in London's most famous teaching hospital which was then all-male – apart of course from the nurses who were all female. In spite of a certain degree of permanent introspection, the fellow seemed fairly normal. He did not indulge in the average medical student's hobbies of drinking and nurses, but though not overtly religious, had once provided a background rumbling noise for some hearty evangelicals who were loudly reciting the marriage service in the early hours of the morning outside the locked bed-sitting room door of a colleague who, some hours previously, had managed to smuggle a particularly beautiful but naïve young nurse into his room. The effect was to undo all the patient hard work the boy had put in and resulted in the confused young maiden leaving hurriedly in a state of dishabille to a joyful chorus of Hallelujahs.

Most of the medical students were obliged to live in 'digs' and travel to and from the hospital by train and those of us lucky enough to live in hospital accommodation were quartered in a run-down building, whose only door opened into a dark and narrow passageway behind the mortuary block. The fact that our tiny, dismal bed-sitting rooms had been condemned as unfit lodgings for the hospital charwomen many years previously did not worry us – at least we were independent. Each room boasted a small window too high to look out of and so encrusted with grime that only the minimal amount of light filtered in from the all-pervading murk of the narrow alleyway outside. It was in this alley that the workmen stored their buckets and paraphernalia and they leant their ladders up against the windowless back wall of the mortuary block, which towered above our little hostel, so that we could not even see any sky from our rooms. A thick coating of soot and grit from the hospital chimney on one's books and papers was the reward for opening a window, whose only use, with the help of a short alley-ladder, seemed to be to admit some nubile young nurse to one's room. This was the portal of entry for any eager, but coy, girl who did not want to run the gauntlet of the permanent cluster of medical students gossiping in the kitchen just inside the only door, and whose desire for bedroom privacy without the marriage service was paramount.

One singularly dull enervating Saturday afternoon in February, I was lying on my bed in the usual semi-darkness sipping Lapsang Souchong, while recovering from the previous evening's moderate excess of Barclay Perkins' extra-special Number Two Doctor brand, my favourite ale, when the door opened. My acquaintance the cadaver came in from the long narrow corridor which of course had to be artificially lit all day and, unable to see anything, he switched on my single 100-watt electric light bulb which hung high and naked from the ceiling. I swore at him as the fierce light exploded in my bloodshot eyeballs and he had the sense to switch it off. He fumbled his way to my rickety wooden chair and sat down, mumbling incoherently. When his hooded eyes became accustomed to the late afternoon gloom of my room, he helped himself to a tooth-mug of oriental tea. Gradually his words strung themselves into phrases, which became almost intelligible, and eventually I realized he was asking me if I would care to join him for a couple of days of hill-walking in North Wales. Anything would be better than this London smog and so I agreed. I understood him to say there was an overnight bus leaving Victoria bus station in four hours time. I had not been to North Wales and imagined the landscape there to be an unfinished copy of the glorious green hills and friendly valleys of West Wales – but how stark and raw a copy I was soon to discover.

After a little more rest and some dry toast, I felt sufficiently recovered to prepare for the journey. But I was certainly not prepared for the sight of a cadaver dressed in sickly-yellow oilskins, carrying a vicious looking navvy's pickaxe, with enough rope wound around his chest and over one shoulder to hang himself and most of the people on the bus, some of whom looked likely candidates for the hempen rope anyway.

Following a nightmare journey through the wild night, I lurched off the bus into the freezing dawn of a rainy day in Chester. There we found two skeletal figures in a rusty corrugated iron lean-to, doling out a bitter, dark orange viscous liquid they called 'tea', and this, together with thick grey bread smeared with some rancid yellow substance, passed as breakfast. Spittoons were provided but no vomit bowls. At the railway station we boarded a train to a small North Wales village, where we were met by a friend of the cadaver; an earnest, elderly man who confessed that a few hours ago a bishop had received him into the Church of England in Wales. This I assumed accounted for the evangelical enthusiasm he displayed as he welcomed us into his neat bungalow, where he cooked passable ham and eggs for us to the strains of Bach's organ music. Like many people who live alone, he seemed over-solicitous for the wellbeing of his guests and even suggested I went to bed for a few hours to recover from the dreadful bus journey, an invitation I politely declined, whereupon a sickly smile split the grey face of my cadaveric acquaintance.

After some more sacred music, a visit to the parish church and some tea and buns, the creepy old man invited my oilskin-clad associate into the passenger seat of his Austin-seven car. As I squeezed into the back seat among the rucksacks, boots, sleeping bag, duvet-jacket, leather jacket, rope and pickaxe, I had recovered sufficiently to realize just how much luggage my colleague had brought for this 'walk'. The car stopped after half an hour's slow, jerky ride along a deserted road through the driving rain and I fell out clutching all my luggage, which consisted of one small khaki haversack containing sponge-bag, pyjamas and pants. The sight of the cadaver wrestling with his luggage prompted me to offer help, though I felt it was his own stupid fault he'd brought so much clobber. The result was that I found myself loaded with a large unwieldy holdall, three huge rucksacks which seemed to contain lead weights, and a dangerously sharp navvy's pickaxe, which I was told was an ice axe. When the car's red rear lights had disappeared into the all-pervading gloom, I realized that it was practically pitch dark and the only sounds were of rain pelting down and the cadaver's slow breathing and disembodied mumbling, which I interpreted as 'follow me'. There was nothing to follow except the clump of his heavy boots on the uneven stony way which seemed to lead uphill as I squelched behind, my lightweight, polished, black town shoes making loud sucking noises at every step.

Eventually we arrived at what appeared to be a derelict stone barn which turned out to be an important centre for mountain rescue. It was, incidentally, also a place where young people could rest before risking their lives, and the lives of those lumbered with the chore of having to rescue them, when they became stranded, helpless, on the menacing mountains of rock I was soon to find surrounded this God-forsaken place. Sitting on the stone floor in a semicircle, around a smoking wood fire, was an assortment of hearty young men and women, some of whom, sooner or later would, no doubt, owe their lives to the two quiet mountain-rescue men playing chess in the corner. Beyond a too-cheery 'hello', no one took the slightest notice of me except the cadaver, who told me I'd have to clear out the grate and lay the fire in the morning, while he swept the floor and made the breakfast, this being the house rule for late arrivals. My lightweight raincoat was not made for such an unrelenting downpour and my skin was rainwashed, whereas the cadaver was dry under his oilskins, so though it was not yet ten o'clock, I decided to go to bed after finding some place to dry my clothes. The facilities were barely primitive and I climbed up onto an unclaimed top bunk, which swayed to and fro under the rafters supporting the leaking roof. Exhausted I fell asleep.

The waving light in front of my face was not part of a dream and, as I raised my hand to shield my eyes, I saw the cadaver standing over me holding a storm lantern and muttering something about making a fire. I could hear healthy snoring all around me in the darkness, so I instructed the cadaver to creep back into his tomb and take his corpse-candle with him. The response was so uncharacteristic of him that it jerked me awake. He pulled the two smelly grey blankets off me and gripping hold of my left thigh muttered what sounded like 'matchstick'. My loud swearing, besides making him back-off, awoke bodies in the surrounding bunks and the menacing noises and threats all around indicated the wisest plan was to get up.

I was in the middle of the filthy job of clearing out the grate and laying the fire, when a series of loud grunts from the kitchen area signalled breakfast was ready. Ater an abortive hand-rinse in icy water in a cracked Belfast sink, I sat down to cold, limp, streaky bacon and stewed, lukewarm tea. No one else was stirring and my vague doubts about my companion began to crystallize. It now appeared that some of the baggage I'd been lugging around also contained togs for me – heavy clodhopping boots with sharp nails in the steel-plated soles, which I was obliged to wear because my shoes were still soggy after last night's downpour, and also a huge lumpish leather coat because my raincoat was soaked through. But I did protest when I had the weight of one hundred foot of thick coiled rope draped across my shoulder and that damned ice axe thrust into my bare hands. The overnight change in the fellow was remarkable. From being a quiet, timid, mumbling nonentity in London, he had become an overbearing, single-minded hulk, whose impassive grey eyes were just visible between his black woollen Balaclava helmet and the high upturned Dracula collar of his massive billowing down-lined hooded jacket. He held open the door to the freezing waste outside, gripping the storm lantern in the other thick wool-mittened hand, and as I stepped out into the blackness I glanced back and caught sight of the wall clock – not yet 6 a.m. My protestations fell on deaf well-covered ears and the storm lantern was already moving away, swaying in the cutting wind. Using the ice axe as a makeshift, most uncomfortable walking stick I managed to keep up with the only friendly thing there was – the kindly light – and I remembered the hymn Cardinal Newman wrote when he left the State Church for the Roman Church, but there was no 'encircling gloom' here, just bloody pitch blackness. The questions I had been too easy-going and polite to ask before, came tumbling out – why an ice axe and why a hundred foot of rope for a walk in the hills? The only intelligible word that floated back to me through the darkness was '. . . prepared'. The way was becoming rougher with rocky outcrops, and my feet began to rebel against the tight unyielding boots I had been constrained to wear.

After about half an hour of increasingly painful walking I fancied there was a subtle change in the echoes of our steel-shod footfalls on the rock. Though I had given up trying to hold any kind of conversation with the hulk ahead, I did remark a few times on my impression and was eventually rewarded with the words 'frozen lake'. I wondered if it might be the lake of the one-eyed fish, but sensed it was the deep lake in which the boy Prince of the Royal House of Wales had drowned a thousand years ago, and over which no bird had since flown. I thought better of mentioning this. Walking was now becoming increasingly difficult and I was reduced to hobbling along behind the lantern light, which was becoming fainter and fainter as it moved relentlessly further and further away, and I started to use the ice axe as a prehensile proboscis, feeling my way between the rocks in the cavernous blackness.

After stumbling and falling on a number of occasions and calling out, to no avail, I decided the only way to get the clod ahead to stop and wait for me was to abuse his precious ice axe, so I raised it high above my head and brought it down in an arc to strike the rock at my feet again and again. The icy clanging sounds ringing across the unseen deep waters reminded me somehow of King Arthur's Sword, the Stone and the Lake, and I started to laugh at my predicament as I recalled that it was only just over thirty hours ago I had been sipping China tea lying comfortably on my bed in London. At last the swaying light stopped and as I limped up to it, I heard a sigh of exasperation before it was off again, though I fancied the pace was a little slower; maybe because of fear that the beloved ice axe might suffer damage from further misuse at the hands of a philistine. And so it went on for an age in the freezing blackness until at last the crank stopped, and by the light of the lantern I saw him slowly draw forth from the inner recesses of his enormous coat a pocket torch, a compass and a chewed-up map. While he pored over his map and compass holding the torch between his teeth, I seized the chance to try to warm my numbed fingers at the lantern. After some incomprehensible muttering we were off again, but in what seemed to be a different direction.

It was some time later, in the grey light of a feeble dawn, that I gradually became aware of my surroundings. A few yards to my right was a vast ice-covered lake stretching away into the murk, enclosed on three sides by perilous ice-bound cliffs of black rock which towered up out of sight above us. As the light began to filter through the gloom, I could see we were at the far end of this narrow lake and that the only way to continue the 'walk', would be to skirt the lake on the other side and end up where we started; or boringly and painfully to retrace our steps. There was no other way out. Stumbling in the dark among rocks on one side of a lake and returning, no doubt between rocks which at least one could now see, on the other side of the lake was not my idea of an enjoyable walk. But as I was soon to discover, walking was not on today's menu. Of course I should have realized that a pleasant stroll among the hills did not call for a hundred feet of rope and an ice axe, and I should have asked much sooner for an explanation, always assuming I would have been able to invest the muttered replies with some meaning. Instead I had left it too late and all I had to go on was the word '. . . prepared', which still echoed in my mind an hour or more after it had been mouthed in the darkness.

He had stopped and was removing the heavy coils of rope from my aching shoulder and the ice axe from the grip of my blue frozen hands. To one side the immense sheet of ice covering the awesome depths of the lake glistened in the unwilling dawn. But even that was more inviting than the menace that towered over me on the other side. The black glassy rock face rose at first gently, but then sheer into the grey clouds hundreds of feet above. Without a word, as though sensing I was seriously considering going back the way we'd come, he tied one end of the rope tightly around my waist and, after uncoiling it, tied the other end to a sort of harness he was wearing around his waist and thighs. Looking back I cannot decide whether I allowed him to tie me to the rope because I was imbued with a youthful sense of adventure, or was afraid of appearing to have cold feet in more ways than one, or was just plain stupid. In any event, without a word he started to climb up the rock face using his hands and feet much as a lame monkey would do, except that no doubt a monkey would have some sane reason for doing it.

As I stood there freezing in my thin cotton trousers while he clambered above me, I could see that he was wearing woollen breeches, thick woollen stockings and canvas gaiters tied under the instep. The higher he climbed the less like a disabled monkey and the more like an overweight beetle trying to negotiate a steeply sloping piece of slippery slate did he look. As he climbed, the rope on the ground went up with him and soon I could just about make out his stationary form fumbling about on a ledge about eighty feet up, as he started to pull up the twenty feet or so of rope still lying on the ground. When it was taut I felt a tug on the rope around my waist and heard a yowl which echoed and re-echoed around the icy crags. I understood this to mean I was to start the undignified manoeuvre myself and, like a baby trying to crawl in spite of being jerked on a rein, I managed to get up the piercingly cold rock face with nothing worse than gashed hands which stopped bleeding almost immediately – not because of a hyperactive blood-clotting mechanism, but simply because the blood must have frozen almost as soon as it was shed. As I used my bone-chilled hands to pull myself onto the ledge I saw that he had tied his ungainly carcass to a jagged piece of rock and was now wearing leather gauntlets over his woollen mittens.

Without a word he grasped the rope around my waist and pulled it round behind me. He then proceeded to tie it to the jagged piece of rock, untied himself and coiled the whole length of rope on what little space there was on the ledge. Then, pointing in the direction of my bloodied hands, he took off his leather gauntlets, handed them to me and muttered what I thought was the word 'bloody'. Touched by this sudden and unexpected show of friendship and fellow-feeling, I shrugged it off saying something to the effect that it was nothing really, just a few scratches, but I was quite unprepared for what followed and almost lost my balance on that narrow ledge as he bellowed "Belay!" in my left ear. I had obviously misinterpreted a word of command for a word of concern for my bloodstained hands. What followed can only be described as a dumb show, which was however accompanied by inarticulate grunts from which I gathered I was to stand with my back to the rock face and, as he climbed the second pitch, I was to pay out the rope with one hand while gripping it with the other. I was to wear the gauntlets

106

so that if he fell I could slow down and arrest his fall, because the rope would then not be torn out of my grip nor, of far less moment, result in friction burns of my hands.

This next pitch was a steep wall of about seventy feet with less obvious handholds and footholds. I became increasingly more concerned as I saw him trying out these various possible holds, which were invisible to me, and hesitate before cautiously testing another, and then another, with his not inconsiderable weight. The higher he climbed the more he looked like an inebriated fly slowly and unsteadily zigzagging up a window pane, and I began to imagine what would happen if he lost his hold. He would come hurtling down and already I could see the whitish-grey brain matter from inside my head oozing over the edge of the ledge, as the ice axe strapped to his waist split open my skull and, as I put my hands up to my head, I could feel the sharp splinters of bone piercing the pulps of my fingers through the gauntlets. However he did not fall, and as I was contemplating how far a globule of brain-substance would have to fall in this arctic air before it froze solid and smashed into a million spiculed cells on the ice of the lake below, I heard an unearthly howl and felt a most unfriendly tug on the rope.

I unbelayed, removed the gauntlets, thrust them inside the leather jacket and turned to face the rock stretching sheer and malignant up to the eyrie where the hooded body perched waiting. I must subconsciously have recalled, and adapted to my climbing, the one-handed method of administering an intravenous injection to a patient, whereby the needle and syringe are held steady on the skin with three fingers while the thumb depresses the plunger; because as I climbed up the winterbound vitreous face of the rock, I found myself holding fast with three limbs and searching for holds with only one hand or foot at a time. This, I learnt later, was the three-point climbing rule. My fingers, which had become warmer in the gauntlets, quickly froze again and when I was about twenty feet above the ledge, my left hand slipped off the piece of rock I was gripping just as my right foot was casting around for a foothold and I was left suspended by my right hand and left foot. Fortunately these were good holds but I was forced to look down between my legs to find somewhere to put my faltering right foot. Up until now I had not allowed myself to look down further than my footholds for fear of losing my nerve. But now I had caught sight of the sharp outcrops on the rock face and the jagged crags a hundred feet below; they were waiting to tear my flesh from my broken bones before I crashed through the ice into the black depths of the lake. It was then that the first wave of real fear welled up and passed silently through me leaving me cold inside. There was no way out. I had, by my own stupidity, allowed myself to get into this life-threatening position, but I took comfort from the thought that it would make a good story when – I dismissed the 'if' – I rejoined civilized company.

But I had been shaken, and found the rest of the climb becoming more and more frightening and consequently more hazardous. I began to lose confidence in my hands and feet and, instead of cursing, I started to repeat what I could remember of the little prayers I had said nightly as a child. Subdued, I ascended painfully until the shelf of rock where the silent one crouched was at eye level. I managed to get both hands onto its sharp edge and, with no help from him, felt around and found a shallow ridge of rock a few feet in from its edge. Pulling hard on my hands I levered my elbows up onto the rim of the ledge. Then using my thigh muscles I dragged my heavily-booted feet up the rock face and, with a tremendous effort, pulled my body up until my heaving rib-cage was on a level with the ledge. Numb from exhaustion and cold, I ended up kneeling on the edge, as if in prayer, facing my tormentor who did precisely nothing to help me regain my feet as I teetered perilously on the edge. Without a word he changed belays and it was then I realized that, since he had given me the only pair of belaying gauntlets, I would be able to slow down any fall of his, but without gauntlets he would be unable to slow down a fall of mine as I went hurtling down.

He had already started up the perpendicular wall of rock while I was still pondering this frightening state of affairs. As I looked upwards and cursed his large woollen-covered behind, I took a perverse pleasure in observing that he was in difficulty. He was about thirty feet above my narrow mantleshelf, leaning backwards with his legs wide apart, uneasily straddling an overhanging bulge in the rock face, and that part of his body from the hips down was jerking violently up and down as though he were in the clonic phase of an epileptic fit. A sound came from him as of a yeti in the second stage of labour and I could see that he was hanging on by his hands while his feet were by now lashing around trying to find footholds. Normally a sensitive sort of chap, I was surprised that I felt no sympathy for him and, quite selfishly and cold-bloodedly, calculated that I was quite safe as he would fall from an overhang which protruded a good wide coffin's width out beyond my mantelshelf, so that I would be out of range of his body and lethal ice axe, as they crashed down past me. However, I was decent enough not actually to want him to lose his grip on the overhang and fall, so I averted my eyes and thought of the head of froth on my favourite ale and other pleasant images. While I was so engaged the brittle air was shattered by ecstatic hooting noises, as though the yeti had delivered itself of its abominable offspring. I looked up, but all I could see was that the thirty feet or so of rope that was curled up on my ledge had started to move slowly upwards over the overhanging rock and, as I took off the belaying gloves, I felt somewhat guilty as I became aware that I had not been holding the rope at all while he was having his clonic spasms.

I was still trying to rationalize what would be considered a dereliction of duty on my part in a coroner's court, when I heard a bellowing noise and the last few feet of rope left on my ledge started to travel upwards at a greatly increased rate. Then came the most unwelcome tug of all on the rope, accompanied by more of his diabolical bellowing. I had already decided I would avoid the overhang by skirting it on the left-hand side, where the rock wall, though perpendicular, appeared to offer an easier route. But during the course of my outflanking manoeuvre the pull on the rope progressively increased, dragging me back over to the right and towards the overhang; this, in spite of my repeated hollering for the tension in the rope to be slackened. I was still unable to see the idiot at the other end of the rope, but when I was within a few yards of successfully negotiating my route and avoiding the hazard, he gave the rope an almighty tug, jerking my feet off the footholds so I was treading air. I remember shouting and being suspended horizontally at right angles to the rock face as I tried desperately to hang on, clawing at the rock with my hands, but the pull on the rope was too strong and my hands were torn from the rock, leaving strips of skin from my bleeding fingers in the handholds.

It is said that at the moment of death one's whole life flashes before one in the twinkling of an eye. There was no sun, but in that instant the surface of the lake

110

was a vast expanse of crystal, shimmering in the red, gold and blue colours of the young Prince, as I plunged headlong into oblivion in the black depths to meet him in death. When I came to, I was swinging like a pendulum at the end of the long rope and trying to fend off the jagged spikes of rock that ripped through my clothes and flesh as I crashed into them again and again, while I swung back and forth in simple harmonic motion; then I lost consciousness again.

Now I was being drawn upwards like a hooked fish on the end of a line, but the line was a rope getting progressively tighter and tighter around my waist and pressing up against my rib-cage, so that breathing was becoming more and more difficult. I remember, as I lapsed into unconsciousness once more, wondering whether perishing in the unfathomable depths of the lake would have been quicker than death from suffocation due to chest compression. Dreaming that I was impaled through the chest on an ice axe, I woke up lying on my back on a rocky ledge. I felt as though my head had been split open; I had pain in every part of my body. Breathing was so difficult that my breaths came in short rapid gasps and when I attempted to sit up I became dizzy, even before I had glanced over the edge and seen the sheer drop of more than two hundred feet to the ice-bound lake below. The silent one was hunched up on the ledge and though I knew that he had probably saved my life, my first words were, "You crazy bastard, you nearly killed me." He did not reply and we sat literally in frozen silence.

At length he handed me a sheathed knife. As I ran my blood-clotted fingers over the shining blade, an awesome thought was dredged up from out of my subconscious; did this weird figure crouching before me expect me to exact a gory retribution and see his blood being spilt on this perilous ledge – this Sacrificial Rock – in this God-forsaken place of ancient human sacrifice? As I suppressed this idea he raised his arm and pointed to the lower left part of his heavy leather coat that I was wearing and, by means of signs and various Neanderthal growls, indicated there was something to eat concealed inside the coat which I was to cut open with the knife. This I did with sadistic pleasure and plunging my hand into the slashed lining I pulled out two eggs. I handed him one. He shelled it and swallowed it whole, as though it were an oyster, and I could visualize the peristaltic waves as it passed slowly down his reptilian gullet. My egg stank like putrefying flesh and with evil satisfaction I hurled it down the way I had very nearly gone myself. Without a word he got up, unbelayed himself and started up the sheer rock face, but before he had climbed more than the height of a tombstone, I had made a firm resolution and I dragged him back down. He swore a foul oath and as I swore back at him I informed him I had had enough of his life-threatening tomfoolery and was going down. In his rage he stamped his steel plated boots on the slippery ledge, lost his balance and as he fell backwards caught his head a resounding crack against the rock. Undeterred he rolled over onto his stomach like a fat brown beetle and had already started back up the precipitous rock face before I yanked him back down again.

His normally-hooded, calculating eyes were by now blazing red, wide with fury, and I began to count my chances in a fight with this committed madman on a perilous ledge with a perpendicular drop of more than two hundred feet to the lake below. I knew that if it came to a scuffle he would be the one to go over the edge because I was safely belayed. As well as that, I still had his knife and knew the time had now come to use it against this lunatic who, I was now convinced, had set out to kill me that black Monday morning on the slaughtering rocks in this wild and desolate lunar landscape. I was holding the rope in my left hand and as he took one step towards me I raised the knife in my right hand. He hesitated, and for the first time looked directly into my face; what he saw must have convinced him that I too had been touched by mountain madness as I brought the knife down onto the rope yelling,

"I'll cut this bloody thing!"

He retreated, both hands in the air and howled like a wolf denied its prey. I knew I had won. Sheathing the knife I unbelayed and lowered myself over the edge clinging on with my hands as I looked down between my legs to find footholds. I knew he would belay because otherwise if I fell I would jerk him down to his death with me. I was as single-minded in my descent as I had been two-minded on the way up and, fortunately for me, did not know that most climbers are killed on the way down. The descent was accomplished in absolute silence. When I reached the lake's edge I untied the rope and left the sheathed knife on a rock; without waiting for company I threaded my way back through the dead landscape in the dull noon-light as quickly as my blistered feet and aching limbs allowed.

Back at base I discovered that my soaking clothes of last night had been dried by a young girl – a beautiful young girl – who told me in her delightful French accent that she was staying here *'un peu plus longtemps'* as an unpaid au pair to try to improve her English. After I had changed, I was genuinely sorry to have to say, "*Non, merci,*" to her kind, "*Voulez-vous une tasse de café au lait?*" because I did not want her to witness the baser side of my nature, which would inevitably surface when the lumbering inmate returned to this nuthouse; so without delay I bade her a fairly fond *au revoir*.

As quickly as I could, I made my way to the road in order to put as much distance as possible between myself and the sinister being I thought might well be stalking me. After I had walked about a mile along the road a bus came towards me and stopped at my request, though the driver looked dubiously at me when I asked to be taken to the nearest centre of civilization, especially since I'd been walking in the wrong direction.

When we arrived at the terminus, which was in a sizeable town, he told me that the only bus back was at 10 p.m. and its last stop would be about six miles from where he'd picked me up. I found a reasonable restaurant where I was served edible food as I browsed through the town's guidebook, which urged visitors not to miss seeing 'the unique moving figure of Christ' in the Church. After a silent prayer of thanks for deliverance from the devil of the heights, I asked a pleasant lady, who was arranging flowers in the church, where I could find the moving figure of Christ. Though she had been a regular attender at this church for twenty-two years she said that she had never seen any figure of Christ that moved, so after a fruitless search I came to the conclusion that the broken wooden figure I found hanging near the west door must have emotionally moved the writer of the guidebook. After exhausting all the places of interest mentioned in the handbook, I was drinking a lonely pint and wondering how to fill the rest of the afternoon and evening before my bus and my five-mile walk, when I was hailed by a young chap who said he had been four years my junior at school. Although I couldn't place him he remembered me well because, as senior prefect on duty one particular day, I had refused to beat a boy sent up for punishment – he was that boy! He insisted on buying me a drink and introduced his student friends to me. After a riotous evening and a fabulously hot Vindaloo

114

curry, I caught the one and only bus and started my five-mile walk in a gloriously happy mood.

It was a cloudless, unseasonably-mild night, peppered with bright stars and I went on my solitary way singing by the light of the full moon. Towards midnight I became aware of voices and when I realized they were calling my name I answered. The result was that some hearties from the bunkhouse where I'd spent last night bore down upon me with torches shouting, "We've got 'im, 'e's OK!"

Then an important person came along and told me off for not having left a message to say where I was going, because a search party was about to leave for the mountains to look for me. In a loud well-lubricated voice I gave vent to my unprintable opinion of the mountains and the boneheads who climbed them, and the effect this had upon the congregation confirmed my suspicions that I was dealing with a sect of Oh-be-Joyfuls. Though I objected to being treated like a sheep that had gone astray, the jolly company marched me back singing uplifting songs in unison and out of tune, which compared very unfavourably with the breezy anthems I had been singing that night. It was hot cocoa and more rousing *Boy's Own* songs squatting on the slate floor when we arrived back at the stone outhouse and I noticed that the cadaver's face was almost alive, but when they became even more zealous in their Hallelujah fervour I slunk out to the kitchen. There I found the lovely French girl sitting with a tiny English-French dictionary, trying to make sense out of a textbook on climbing. Naturally I helped her. She wanted to know all about my experiences during yesterday's early morning 'walk' so I told her; at the same time I learnt from the book that climbs were graded from Easy (Grade I) to Very Severe (Grade VI) and that the body-being-born-again in the next room had, on my very first encounter with rockclimbing, taken me on a Severe (Grade IV) climb. It soon became apparent that she and I shared the same feelings about the holier-than-thou group on the other side of the wall and to escape we wandered out into the star-studded night.

What a difference from eighteen hours ago! The way was smooth and easy under the full moon; the night was almost balmy. As we skirted the lake the treacherous crags of rock loomed up and blocked out some of the starlight, but the moon was still with us. Now, the vast ice-covered lake was our own enchanted rink burnished with silver, inviting us to step into its shining surface and slide, like the carefree children we had become. We did. We slid and skated circling hand in hand until we reached the very centre of our magic lake, and we were all but dancing when the first shudder in the ice-sheet brought us to a halt; the ominous sounds of ice cracking rose to a crescendo, booming and thundering as they echoed and re-echoed around the walls of black rock that towered over us and a huge sheet of ice that had been our platform became detached and slowly sank under us. We were sucked down as if in slow motion into the tightening embrace of the waters of the lake. As our ice-sheet went down into the depths I found myself treading water.

But the girl had been sucked down right underneath the thick table of ice surrounding the gaping hole. Taking a deep breath I launched myself down under the edge of the ice and fortunately soon found her. With a firm grip under her pert bottom and using my legs and free arm, I brought her from under the roof of ice and then propelled us both upwards until our heads were above water. Although she twined her arms and thighs around me while she regained her breath, I found it quite easy to stay afloat lying backwards on the

116

water using my hands and feet like flippers; but when she looked down at me and suddenly kissed me I lost my equilibrium. She uncoiled herself and swam away; for the first time I was able to see how large an expanse of water had been exposed by the sunken sheet of ice and I was surprised how warm the water was. Hampered by my sodden clothes I swam across the lake to where she was treading water and trying to divest herself of her jacket. We helped one another and flung our outer garments onto the gleaming ice surface where, by mutual consent and help, they were soon followed by the rest of our clothes. I would have climbed Mount Everest for what followed. Swimming free in our remote mountain lake, I can still hear her excited cries ringing silver on the brittle air as I chased and caught her again and again.

But it was not until we left the water and were standing at the lake's edge in the glow of that exquisite night that I saw her in all her beauty. She tossed back the wet tresses of her long fair hair and tilted her face to the velvet sky holed by stars; their light sparkled in her eyes as she stood erect, still as a marble statue, confident of her perfect figure. The moonlight gleamed white on her high rose-tipped breasts, glistened on the rivulets of water running down her back towards her slim hips and the tight cleft between her neat buttocks, as she stood clean-limbed with her long legs slightly parted, proud and radiant as a youngster who's just won a race. Exposed to the chill air we looked for and found shelter deep inside a smooth recess; we sought and found warmth in one another.

The moon was low in the sky, the stars had grown faint and a cold mist began to roll over the silent lake as we lay at peace after our mutual acts of worship, our quiet breathing the only sound in the silence of that celestial night.

But gradually I became aware of a faint shuffling sound as though something was moving among the boulders behind our sanctuary. Gently disengaging myself from her sleeping form, I crept stealthily towards the sound, but I'd been seen and from behind a large boulder the thing stood up, turned and fled – it was the corpse. Enraged, forgetting I was naked, I gave chase but almost immediately gashed my bare foot on a splinter of rock and fell. Knowing I would now never catch up with him, I limped back to where she lay curled up like a contented child, unaware that a heathen had been at the leper-squint, while we were communicants at the shining altar. Very gradually and quite unaccountably a feeling of pity for the heathen began to form in my mind. I resolved to keep the contemptible action of the loathsome creature to myself. As I gathered up our wet clothes she stirred, and turning onto her back she stretched her lovely limbs up to me. But for me the spell was broken.

Our shirts were fairly dry and I placed them over her shoulders, draping our two wet jackets over them. We wore our shoes and I put on my wet trousers, but somehow our underclothes had disappeared. She clutched the rest of our clothes to her, while I knelt for her to straddle my neck and shoulders. I felt her moist heat about me as I carried my precious burden down to the little stone shelter where no one, not even the Peeping Tom, was awake.

Today, Tuesday, was the day of return to London, but my disdain for the fellow who had brought me here impelled me to take an early bus to avoid having to travel with him, and incidentally also, to give the miss to his creepy friend in his prim bungalow. The tedious journey yielded two sonnets – one expressing pity for those who, impervious to the beauty of living nature, have to seek out and conquer her dead skeleton, and the other for the eyes of my French girl alone. I received no reply to my letters.

Many years passed before I learnt by chance that the day I went away a fair-haired young girl left for '*Le Rocher des Sacrifices*', and it was assumed she was returning home. The appearance of two clean-cut holes – one very large, one quite small – in the sheet of ice covering the lake was considered a natural phenomenon.

HIS WONDERS TO PERFORM

Donald and I were budding gynaecological surgeons at a military hospital. It was springtime, we were in our twenties, of equal seniority, and most of our patients were the wives of officers and other ranks together with members of the Women's Armed Services. We alternated our outpatient clinics so that a patient attending weekly would see Donald one week and myself the next week. This arrangement worked well until one afternoon a very attractive teenage girl came to my clinic in great distress. She was the only child of working-class parents and had been granted 72 hours compassionate leave a few weeks ago to attend her father's funeral, and was now attempting, on her meagre pay, to support her widowed, semi-invalid mother. Joan was an innocent who had never been away from home before and had joined the armed forces a few months ago straight from cadet school. She had had her first taste of alcohol at a party in the sergeants' mess and had been seduced by a married man, since when she had not had a period.

Donald had seen her last week, had told her she was pregnant and was in danger of miscarrying because her womb was displaced backwards. In order to prevent a miscarriage he had digitally manipulated her womb into the correct position, causing her pain and embarrassment, and to maintain this position he had inserted a large black vulcanite pessary high up in her vagina. This is a painful procedure in an unmarried girl and even more so when performed by someone as taciturn as Donald with his huge square hands. He had told her to return to his clinic in two weeks. However she had suffered great discomfort and pain due to this large foreign body lodged high up inside her and had returned a week early on account of the pain. She had in fact caused herself to bleed when she had tried unsuccessfully to remove it. In those days it was a criminal act to procure or attempt to procure an abortion or miscarriage except in very specifically defined circumstances. She was too frightened to confide in anyone and her seducer had disowned her. She had tried the various common so-called abortifacient drugs without effect and was tearful and upset.

Even in those days it was generally accepted that in the majority of cases backward displacement of a uterus, gravid by less than twelve weeks, corrected itself spontaneously and therefore posed little increased risk of miscarriage. However, my colleague for some reason wanted to make absolutely sure she did not miscarry and so had inserted the pessary. I considered that the pessary should be removed and this I did as gently as I could, whereupon she experienced a deep feeling of relief, and the uterus fell backwards into its original position. I advised and reassured her as best I could and made an appointment for her to come and see me in my clinic in two weeks.

However, she was under the impression that she had to keep her original appointment as well and so turned up at Donald's clinic the following week. That evening the nursing sister who had been in attendance at Donald's clinic told me that he had been very annoyed that I had removed the pessary; he had caused Joan a great deal of pain and distress when he had repositioned the uterus and thrust the large unyielding pessary as far up her vagina as he could with his large spade-like hands. This was completely unnecessary and, acting on the precept that no patient should be the worse for seeing a doctor, I confronted Donald in private that evening and told him so.

I was totally unprepared for his sanctimonious reply spoken in his black bible voice, "She has sinned in the eyes of the Lord."

Having been brought up never to enter into an argument involving religion or politics, I merely said, "Judge not, that ye be not judged."

But even as I said it, I began to wonder if Donald had perhaps misread the first page of her case notes, which merely consisted of a form often filled in by a female medical orderly; if so his heavy-handed efforts might inadvertently have actually proved her salvation. With this in mind I made my way as quickly as I could to the clinic, unlocked the cabinet containing patients' notes, extracted Joan's file and studied her case history notes. My suspicions were confirmed – her periods were regular, but occurred every 23 days instead of the usual 28 days and Donald had misread '23' as '28', so when he had repositioned the uterus and reinserted the pessary that afternoon, he had thought he was doing so more than a week after her third missed period, at which time in the menstrual cycle it is quite safe to carry out gentle uterine manoeuvres; whereas in fact he had performed his ham-fisted manipulations of the uterus on precisely the first day of her fourth suppressed period. Now the very time to avoid any uterine manipulation in early pregnancy is at the time of a missed period, especially on the first day of a missed period, because it is at that time that the uterus is most likely to object and empty itself. I admit that it was with an unholy smile I put the file back in the cabinet and locked up.

Four days later I was on in-take duty taking my turn as hospital orderly medical officer, when I received a call at lunchtime from the sister on emergency duty to see a young girl. It was Joan. She had started bleeding during the night and now had abdominal pains. She had a threatened miscarriage which, on thorough examination, rapidly became an inevitable miscarriage necessitating evacuation of the uterus. Since I had an operating session that afternoon I had her admitted to the gynaecological ward and added her name to my theatre list. It was Donald's turn that week to assist me, and after the three major cases Joan, fully anaesthetized, was wheeled in on a trolley. He did not recognise her with the anaesthetic mask over her face and a theatre cap covering her fair hair and most of her forehead. She was lifted onto the operating table and two nurses flexed her hips and knees, spread her thighs and fixed her feet in the stirrups in the lithotomy position. It was at this point just before the nurses covered her up with sheets that Donald, recognising a birthmark on her left thigh, protested that this was the girl he was treating for retroverted gravid uterus.

"Not any more," I said, but spared him the humiliation of telling him why until we were alone. I took my seat, Donald standing on my right, theatre sister on my left and started the operation. I was halfway through the procedure when suddenly a very loud and insistent wailing noise echoed and re-echoed ominously around the theatre. It was the alarm signal and it wasn't a practice because we as senior officers had not received prior warning.

I carried on with the operation, but when I extended my right hand for the next instrument to be placed in it, nothing happened and I was just about to tell Donald to wake up, when I turned and found he wasn't standing at my right side where he should have been – in fact he wasn't in theatre at all, and neither was anybody else. Even the anaesthetist had disappeared. I heard the sounds of running feet and of heavy objects being manhandled in the corridors; Donald was shouting orders above the clanging and all-pervading howl of the siren. I went to the door and, to avoid desterilising my gloves, pushed it open with my foot.

There was chaos outside the theatre. Nursing orderlies were colliding with one another as they ran backwards and forwards up and down the long corridors. There was an almighty traffic jam in the doorway of the emergency operating theatre. Servicemen acting as amateur porters were struggling to manhandle the old operating table, anaesthetic machine, mobile theatre lamps and other paraphernalia out of that theatre; in the process they were becoming hopelessly entangled with a gang of civilian porters, who were trying to push and lift brand new replacements in the opposite direction into the emergency theatre. The whole seething mass of cursing porters and other ranks seemed to be under the command of Donald, wild-eyed and white-faced, bellowing above the howl of the siren and the crashing of heavy metal anaesthetic gas cylinders as they fell to the floor. Not knowing what was happening I turned back to the safety of my operating theatre, and was able to finish the operation before the patient started to come round from the anaesthetic. Matching the maniacal unreality of the scene outside, I went into the corridor and unceremoniously grabbed hold of two protesting female nursing orderlies, marched them into the operating theatre where I superintended them while they removed the patient's feet from the stirrups, adjusted the table and laid her supine. I then positioned them one on either side of the patient, and warned them they would be on a charge if she rolled off the operating table as she recovered consciousness.

The pandemonium had now moved outside the hospital building and, since in those days operating theatres had windows, I was now free to watch the noisy proceedings outside, though I still had no idea what was going on, neither did the two orderlies. The window looked out past the guard room to the road where the railway line crossed it, and I was surprised to see the commanding officer being chauffeured in his official limousine, pennant flying, with motor cycle outriders, followed by a cavalcade of service cars each containing one administrative officer; these clerks were followed by cars bulging with medical officers representing all the specialities in the hospital except obstetrics, gynaecology and paediatrics. Hot on the trail of the medical officers came three cars turgid with nursing sisters. Bringing up the rear of this procession were three ambulances and about five gigantic transport lorries. Just as this impressive convoy, bristling with brass, was about to cross the railway line, the level crossing gates closed and the cavalcade was forced to a halt.

The portly adjutant eased himself out of his car and, flanked by the burly outriders, did his pathetic best to make it at the double to the signal box, cheered on by the medical officers. First checking that my patient was all right, I opened one of the theatre windows and heard a loud angry shouting match between military personnel and a representative of British Rail, but it was difficult to make out what was being said. I did catch the words 'crash' and 'Edinburgh', and from high up in the signal box the words 'express' and 'piss off' and also 'stupid bastards'. It appeared that the signalman was being ordered to open the gates to let the convoy through. The gesticulating adjutant was joined by three or four beetroot-faced, immaculately uniformed hospital administrators who worked hard from nine to five, Monday to Friday, sending bits of paper from one room to the next, and who would blench at the sight of a cut finger. I was most impressed by the bravery of these clerks who stood glaring up at the signalman's window and shaking their delicate fists. The signalman closed his window and no doubt also locked the door at the top of the wooden steps outside his box.

I noted with satisfaction that not one of the twenty or so medical officers, who were crammed into three cars, deemed it necessary to make a spectacle of himself by taking part in this undignified slanging match. By now the administrators had been joined by some of the hulking lorry drivers whose language was quite robust. One of them was actually climbing up a drainpipe and had almost reached the signalman's window, when a sudden loud piercing whistle accompanied by the thunder of an express train passing within yards of him made him lose his grip, and he fell heavily to the ground. When they found he was unable to stand, one of the senior administrators, without even consulting his book of rules, sent for one of the junior administrators, and having heard the gobbledegook so often I'm fairly confident he ordered him to 'summon assistance of accessible service personnel for urgent non-combatant duties and activate contingency plan III subsection (d)'. In any event, two of the medical officers were already on their way and as a result of examination of the man sent a runner to one of the ambulances, which arrived with its siren shrieking and headlamps flashing according to regulations. The man was placed on a stretcher and brought back the few hundred yards to the hospital accompanied by the full panoply of lights, siren and an escort of two motorcyclists also with headlights flashing, although the road was clear apart from our own service vehicles and a few inquisitive cows.

The railway crossing gates were just opening and the commanding officer's limousine was already accelerating across the line, when another service motorcyclist, horn blaring, lights flashing skidded to a halt alongside the adjutant's car and handed him a dispatch. Ten seconds later the adjutant's car took off seemingly in an attempt to catch up with the CO's limousine, which had by now gathered momentum and was hurtling away down the road at speed and was soon out of sight. Taking their cue and eager not to be left behind, the whole crocodile of cars, ambulances and lorries accelerated and the roaring noise was such that, closing one's eyes, one could imagine a squadron of Lancaster bombers coming in to land.

At any rate the noise seemed to wake up my patient who asked, in one of her lucid intervals of returning consciousness, where we were taking her in the aeroplane, whereupon we assured her it was all over and we were taking her back to the ward. Sure enough, as soon as she was safely back in the care of the gynaecological ward sister, I was asked, as one of the only doctors left in the hospital, to see the signal box mountaineer. When I arrived in the casualty department, a girlfriend of his, a bright young wireless telegraphist, her face pink with giggling, was leaving, having as I thought come to make sure her boyfriend was not seriously hurt, but there was more to it than that. The fellow had broken his leg and after he had been made comfortable, told me his girlfriend's story.

It was an open secret that the Duke of Edinburgh was learning to fly at a nearby aerodrome, but it was not so well known that within a certain radius, selected hospitals were alerted when he took off and put on stand-by when he landed safely. In the event of a crash, mobile units from the nearest hospital would rush to the scene. That afternoon the hospital had received an incorrect signal which, when decoded, indicated that a VIP had crashed a few miles away from our hospital; but a breakdown in the hospital and car radio linkage had meant that the order countermanding mobilisation had to be personally delivered, and did not reach the adjutant until the commanding officer was already speeding away across the railway line.

I learnt later that the adjutant's car had failed to catch up with the CO's limousine, which was eventually brought to a halt by one of our daredevil motorcyclists under orders. He had had to engage in a running battle with one of the CO's motorcycle escorts which resulted in one of them landing in hospital with a broken arm and concussion. The CO's chauffeur was so unnerved by this hair-raising episode that, when he was peremptorily ordered to return to base, he reversed the limousine into a deep ditch full of water at the side of the road, so that its front wheels were off the ground and its long bonnet with its pennant flying pointed skywards. The CO was obliged to remain seated below the road surface, unable to get the door opened, as the muddy water level rose in the gently sinking passenger compartment of the long limousine. He had no choice but to remain in this undignified position while his whole retinue drove past tittering. He was an unpopular CO and it was as though he were taking the salute in a comic opera. The chauffeur, who was waving the cavalcade on, halted the last of the forty-ton service vehicles whose driver was given the unenviable task of hauling the CO in his limousine out of the morass. This accomplished, the convoy made its way back to the hospital in high spirits, though the administrators in their cars looked decidedly po-faced. The heavy transport lorries had had to go a further two miles down the road before they found a place where they could turn.

Those who inadvertently smirked as the CO's mud-spattered limousine passed the guard room were put on a charge for insubordination, as were those who were unable to conceal a smile and forgot to salute when the CO stepped out, his soaking wet uniform trousers clinging to his legs as he dripped evil-smelling muddy water.

The bar in the officers' mess was more lively than

usual that evening, but I must admit I felt pretty smug, not having been involved in the afternoon's ludicrous exercise. But I felt even more smug when I reminded Donald later that one of the best ways of avoiding mistakes in medicine, is to pay great attention to the details in a patient's history, and this time it was my turn to give him a quote – granted it was not from the Bible but from William Cowper – 'God moves in a mysterious way'; he knew the next line.

MARMADUKE'S KNEECAP

We were young doctors at a military hospital and the only one of us who had a car was Marmaduke. But he was not really one of us. The fair had arrived for three days in the little town ten miles away, and that glorious summer evening seven of us had changed into civvies because we wanted to go to the fair. There were no buses and we could expect no help from the transport officer, who had kept reappearing at our various outpatient clinics, complaining of vague lower bowel symptoms and expecting further examinations though there was nothing physically wrong with him. He had taken a dislike to doctors since one of us, referring to his bowel, had told him he had a kink.

There was nothing for it but to ask Marmaduke if he'd lend us his car. We found him in his room listening on his expensive hi-fi apparatus to Mahler's *Das Lied von der Erde* and, as we expected, he refused. So we made ourselves at home. We sat on his bed, on the available chairs and on his table, while we chatted amongst ourselves about the various talents of the female nursing staff, until he realized his quiet musical evening was over. At last, to get us out of his room he agreed, with bad grace, to drive us to the fair in the expensive open sports car his recently knighted father, surgeon at a famous hospital, had given him. Much to his annoyance we clambered all over it and some of us sat on the retracted hood.

Arriving at the fair we made for the dodgem-cars, but it transpired Marmaduke had not been to a fair before, nor heard of dodgem-cars, but we eventually managed to persuade him to ease his six-foot-three-inch frame into a car painted in garish fluorescent purple and pink. In all we commandeered eight cars, and the seven of us proceeded to drive like maniacs in all directions treating them as bumper-cars, not dodgem-cars. The all-pervading insistent throb of the amplified pop music blaring out of the loudspeakers, the flashing red, green and blue lights, the screaming of girls and the yelling of local lads aiming wildly for head-on collisions all added to the simple, vicarious delights of the evening. Under the stroboscopic, multicoloured lighting I glimpsed Marmaduke's car being repeatedly jolted and out of control, revolving about its own axis, a victim of the chaos of cars, his face taut, his knees wide apart wedged tight up against the rim of the car on either side of the steering wheel.

Suddenly a high-pitched shriek cut through the cacophony of sound. Marmaduke, his arms flailing, was trying to stand up in his revolving car but lost his balance and fell full length onto the floor of the rink, his long blond hair a rainbow in the kaleidoscope of lights. The power was immediately switched off, the noise and flashing lights ceased, and in the silence everyone steered their slowing cars away from the prostrate figure. We leapt out of our cars and were joined at Marmaduke's side by the fellow in charge of the dodgems, who wanted to send for a local doctor. We had some difficulty persuading him that all seven of us were doctor colleagues of the victim. As for Marmaduke, he was fully conscious and his first words as he tried to stand up were, "Get me out of this vulgar place!" We helped him to his feet and as he limped out of the rink he let the side down by berating everyone in a loud supercilious voice.

His right kneecap was painful where it had been rammed hard up against the rim of his car as a result of a head-on bump from another car. One of our members was in training as an orthopaedic specialist and in his opinion, which he didn't share with Marmaduke, there was no clinical evidence of bony injury to the knee, so we took him to his car, raised his leg, made him comfortable and, telling him we'd be back in an hour or so, we started back to the fairground.

It was fortunate that one of us happened to turn round and saw that Marmaduke had already driven his car out of the car park and was waiting for a gap in the traffic to get onto the main road. The sight of seven young officers sprinting at top speed across the car park, prompted by the alternative of a ten-mile walk, would have brought joy to the heart of any SAS physical training instructor. We just made it and flung ourselves onto his car as he was accelerating away. He was in a petulant mood and told us it would have served us right if we'd had to walk back for taking him to such a 'sordid place' and it was our fault that he'd injured his knee.

Looking back, I think it was at that moment that we made the unspoken, unanimous decision to teach this spoilt brat a lesson. Since he was driving, he was of course in charge until we arrived back at the hospital, but from then on the course of events was completely unrehearsed.

Not one of us knew how to operate the X-ray machines, but we took him to the radiology department and put up a good pretence of taking an X-ray picture of his knee. He refused to take his trousers off for the X-ray, but let us roll his trouser leg up well above the knee. There was an unexpected flash and a few lights fused, but he did not seem to realize that we had no idea what we were doing. While we made him comfortable on the X-ray couch, our trainee bone specialist went into an adjoining room and ferreted out an old X-ray picture of a fractured kneecap with a large transverse gap between the two fragments. After clipping it into a frame which obliterated the name of the patient and the date, he dipped it into a tank of fixing solution so as to wet it and make it appear the film had just been developed. When Marmaduke saw it he became even more objectionable and accused us of deliberately setting out to injure him, even though neither he, nor any one of us, knew who had actually delivered the blow which he was now convinced had fractured his kneecap. To our amazement he seemed to be unaware that he would have been quite unable to drive the car if he had indeed sustained the type of fractured kneecap we'd shown him on the X-ray picture. Neither did he seem to realize that his continued vituperation was merely serving to harden our resolve to bring him to heel and to make him pay for ruining our evening, because in fact, all that was wrong with him was a superficial graze on his knee.

It was then that our novice bone-setter stated in a loud voice so that Marmaduke could hear, that he had once seen an operation where, after scraping away the blood clot with a sharp spoon, the orthopaedic surgeon had drilled holes in the fragments of the fractured kneecap and had then approximated and fixed the fragments in position using kangaroo tendon, threaded through the drill holes. Because we had no kangaroo tendon, our amateur 'orthopod' said we'd have to use silver wire which, though not as good because it caused rarefaction of the bone and worked loose, would be all right as a temporary patch-up job. One of our members had administered a few general anaesthetics under close supervision, and volunteered to anaesthetize Marmaduke for the operation. The effect was electric.

From lying supine on the couch verbally abusing us, this son of a well-known surgeon became, in an instant, a wild animal, springing off the couch and racing down the corridor cursing and yelling which, if further proof were needed, confirmed to us that there was really nothing wrong with him. We brought him down with a rugby tackle and he fought like a tiger as we manhandled him down to the operating theatre. It took five of us to hold him down on the operating table while he was stripped completely in preparation for the operation, which of course we had never intended to perform because his kneecap was intact, and even if it were fractured, a week's rest would be necessary to allow tissue-swelling to subside before operation; but he didn't know that. The cumbersome anaesthetic machine with its heavy clanking gas cylinders was wheeled in, and he was told that because he was so obstreperous, anaesthesia could not be induced by the normal pleasant injection method but would have to be induced by the less agreeable inhalation method. It was when he heard the hiss of the gases and the rubber mask was placed over his face that he broke down and pleaded with us to leave him alone.

Being reasonable people we agreed not to anaesthetize him, nor to subject him to any form of surgery, so long as he agreed to being immobilized in plaster, but we omitted to mention how much of him we proposed to immobilize, or how much plaster we intended to use. He was only too ready to agree to anything in order to avoid surgery under general anaesthesia, and so we took him to the plaster room where there were literally hundreds of yards of plaster of Paris bandages of various widths just waiting to be used. We drew a piece of wide stockinette over his head and shoulders to cover him from his lower ribs to his groins, and narrower pieces to sheathe his legs and thighs. Fortunately he did not realize we were subjecting him to quite the wrong treatment as we transferred him into a special metal frame and suspended him horizontally by his head, shoulders and hips from the overhead beam. We fixed his feet to metal sole-plates, and with so little evidence of support, he looked, from a distance, as though he were practising levitation. Normally all bony points around the hips and spine are covered with pads of cotton wool for comfort, but Marmaduke was so well-upholstered we thought this unnecessary, and so the plastering began in real earnest.

Two of us were fully employed soaking the plaster bandages in hot water, salted to make the plaster set quicker, then handing them to the plasterers, who used far more bandages than were necessary and plastered him thickly and thoroughly from his waist down both thighs and legs to his toes, leaving only a small keyhole-shaped gap between the tops of his thighs. He complained that we were immobilizing far more than his right kneecap, but kept quiet when we threatened to take him back to the operating theatre. This huge mass of plaster set into a very heavy cast an inch thick, and when he was released from the frame he was barely able to move even with crutches. We escorted him to his ground floor room in the officers' mess and found a bucket which we left at the side of his bed.

The next morning as I was leaving the mess, after a late and solitary breakfast, I caught sight of Marmaduke half-lying in the reclining driving seat of his car, while his batman seemed to be adjusting his feet on the pedals of the car. Apparently he'd sent for one of the plaster room attendants, and had him remove sufficient plaster from his right foot so that he could use the accelerator and brake pedals, which was all he needed as the car had automatic transmission. He told me he was driving to London to see his father, who he'd been unable to contact by telephone because he was chairing an international surgical conference. Then he mentioned the name of the leading orthopaedic surgeon in the country, also a knight, who was his father's yachting companion, and who would no doubt be taking over Marmaduke's treatment. As though that wasn't enough good news, Marmaduke then informed me that his father was also consulting surgeon to the armed services holding the highest rank.

It was at this point that I tore back up the steps to the mess and put out emergency calls for the other six doctors to join me, only to hear the sound of a car engine starting up. I just managed to reach the car as it was moving off and stopped it by snatching the key from the ignition. Cursing, Marmaduke ordered his batman to get the key back from me. I had no alternative but to 'pull rank' and, countermanding Marmaduke's order, dismissed the batman, whereupon Marmaduke informed me that he would see to it, via his father, that I was court-martialled and dismissed the service. This information on my curriculum vitae would ensure a bleak future for me, and I saw myself a stowaway in the hold of a cargo boat ploughing through the seas on my way to a banana republic, hoping to find work as a mortuary attendant – assuming they had mortuaries. All my colleagues, except for the two who were scrubbed-up in theatre, arrived within minutes to be told they too would be facing courts-martial.

Marmaduke was still reclining in his seat, his plump cheeks large pink bellows puffing in and out and it was then I realized how ludicrous the whole situation had become, with a third of the medical staff of this famous military hospital facing possible dismissal with ignominy, on account of a schoolboy prank – or was it? And when Marmaduke found out there was no fracture, would his father's wrath mean we would all be shot at dawn!

Rummaging around under the inlaid mahogany dashboard he had found the spare ignition key, and was slyly inserting it when it was deftly removed from his grasp, giving rise to more cursing and even more dire threats. We all knew that the sooner we told him the truth the better, but should we tell him before or after removing the plaster? We decided on the former since, though flabby, he was of powerful build, and might require considerable physical restraint when he was told, and this would be much easier if he were in a plaster cast. He refused our help to get out of his car, but eventually had to accept it, and we steered him to his room and thoughtfully provided him with three fingers of brandy before telling him; but the force with which he hurled the glass and its contents against the wall served to confirm our decision to keep him hobbled until, and maybe for some time after, he was told the truth.

Whether we were feeling collective remorse or whether no one individual wanted the now dubious honour of being dubbed as last night's ringleader, I don't know, but it was as a result of numerous subtle references to horseplay at school and in the services, that he eventually asked the question, "Is my patella fractured or not?" No one answered but someone started to tell the story of how, disguised in high ranking military uniform, I had carried out an unheralded inspection of one of the smaller military hospitals in the absence of its commanding officer, and had been saluted by all the medical officers at every turn. The whole point of the story was that no one was any the worse off, the idea being that this could now apply to Marmaduke's kneecap. But he wasn't to be mollified; in fact he was furious, and when he started flinging heavy books and china and anything within reach at us, we decided not to overstay our welcome, but to call again in a few hours when he had become more reasonable. Our plan was to apologize and be nice to him and, if he behaved decently, we were even willing to admit him to our circle. But that was not to be.

The seven of us arrived at his room soon after lunch, but Marmaduke had disappeared leaving the cumbersome plaster cast, now split longitudinally in two like the lower part of the mummy case of Tutankhamun. That afternoon we scoured the hospital and the whole of the camp, but were unable to find him. We discovered later that he had been with the commanding officer making an official complaint about his fellow officers, and demanding a redress of grievances. He got it. Within the week he was posted to one of the most unpopular postings in the armed services and we heard no more.

THE SNOW CAESAR

I was about a third of the way up the ladder to obtaining a consultancy in obstetrics and gynaecology and was very happy in my post as registrar in the specialty at a modern hospital boasting all the latest equipment. It had been meticulously planned and had been built on two floors only, so as not to obtrude unduly into its delightful rural surroundings. Terraced lawns with goldfish ponds and sparkling fountains led up to the imposing main entrance hall which would have done justice to a luxury hotel. An army of gardeners attended to the extensive, beautifully kept grounds that surrounded the hospital. The doctors and nursing staff worked harmoniously and took pride in the care given to our patients. In those days we were unencumbered by the continual petty interferences of profit-orientated, gobbledegook-speaking office boys and clerks, nowadays known as 'hospital administrators'. The hospital chiefs were the Medical Superintendent, who was himself an eminent doctor, and the Matron, a wise and well-respected lady who lived in a flat overlooking the terraced gardens, and somehow seemed to know everything that went on in the hospital by day and by night. At that time hospitals were run for the benefit of the patients and not for the benefit of the State.

I had been informed, albeit *sotto voce*, on my appointment as registrar that during my two-year term of office I would be expected to spend three months, divided into two periods of six weeks each (and I soon found out why) at an outlying hospital 'up the valleys'

141

where I would be single-handed. This was in marked contrast to the state of affairs here at the base hospital where, as registrar, I supervised the four resident junior doctors in my specialty. I was, of course, also resident in the hospital, as were all registrars everywhere in the three major medical specialties in which urgent life-saving action might be required at any time of day or night. I had a large, deeply-carpeted, well-furnished bedsitting room with a bedside telephone and washbasin, and my windows overlooked the lawns and fountains at the front of the hospital with splendid views of the rolling countryside beyond. I had two nights a week and one weekend in three off-duty, when I was able to leave the hospital and pass through the lodge gates to the world outside, and at these times my Chief, the Consultant Obstetrician and Gynaecologist, would stand in for me. Life was good. Young, uniformed maids brought me tea in bed every morning, cleaned my shoes, saw to my laundry and helped me keep my room and myself in some sort of shape. Most of the nurses and some of the sisters were young, attractive and fun loving and many's the game of tennis we played on the hospital tennis courts, where of course we could be 'on call'. I'm told that the huge tennis tournament cup, which used to sit in the doctors' dining room, is still there with my name and the hospital secretary's name inscribed on it, commemorating the year we won the championship. He was a great guy and extremely efficient in the way he and a few clerks unobtrusively dealt with all the dull business and clerical work of the hospital – I cannot imagine any hospital doctor truthfully writing that now, because today the work of the hospitals is impeded by a plague of self-propagating, pin-striped administrators. There are now more administrators than there are hospital beds. Yes, those were the golden days of summer; they merged gently

142

into the halcyon days of the winter solstice with their indoor sports.

But this could not last. Soon after Christmas the call came and I had to pack my green Standard-8 car with everything I'd need for the next six weeks and, with the sincere commiserations of my friends and hospital colleagues, I set off on my twelve-mile journey into the outback not knowing what to expect. Soon I'd left the countryside behind and, after passing through a busy little town, took the road 'up the valleys', between rows of tiny terraced houses, dwarfed by tall, dismal dilapidated buildings and menacing black coal tips. Reaching a fork in the road, dense with dereliction, I remembered my instructions to take the left fork leading up the larger valley which became more and more ugly and depressing. The road narrowed and snaked between the seemingly never-ending rows of two-up and two-down toy houses all strung tightly together like cheap beads on a little girl's necklace. The front doors, a few brightly coloured as though in protest, opened directly onto the narrow, irregular pavement, chalked with circles, squares and numbers demonstrating that the children had nowhere else to play. These wretched rows of Lego-like houses had been thrown up in terraces by the philistine owners of the coal mines, and climbed up the sides of what must have been a beautiful valley before the invasion of the slavedrivers, whose sole interest was to make as much money as quickly as possible out of the mines, whatever the cost in human misery.

My depression gradually gave way to a feeling that I had embarked on a strange adventure, and I became more and more curious and somewhat intrigued as to the outcome. But nothing had prepared me for my first view of the hospital with its grim forbidding seried ranks of buildings that had been flung haphazardly up the mountainside, whose summit the mist had shrouded as though in shame at the violation. A tortuous tarmacked way zigzagged up and up between the unfriendly buildings as though uncertain of where it was going into the mists. A bedraggled hospital porter directed me to the doctors' residence in the maternity block which was enshrouded in mist, and I had to engage first gear to persuade my friendly little car to take me up there against its will. There was only one other doctor but I didn't see him for a few days. He was a virile young Pakistani with a carefully trained moustache. The residence itself consisted of two tiny bedrooms, one each, a combined lavatory and bathroom emitting a strong scent of musk oil. There was also a small, evil-smelling sitting room with an aerial view of row upon grey row of slate roofs as far as one could see in the all-pervading gloom.

All I could see through my bedroom window at the back of the residence was a high retaining brick wall which effectively blocked out the daylight, but probably prevented the steep, threatening mountainside sliding into my bedroom. The furniture consisted of one ancient, rickety, narrow, metal bedstead with a solid mattress, together with a cheap pine chest of drawers with most of the drawer knobs missing and one simple upright wooden chair with one very short leg. A single naked 40-watt clear electric light bulb hanging from the centre of the lofty ceiling provided the only illumination. I made a mental note that it was too high for me to reach to change it, even if I were foolhardy enough to put the chair on the concrete mattress and somehow wedge the short leg against the wall and risk my neck standing on the tattered wickerwork seat of the chair; the stone floor would not be very welcoming if I fell. Even if I had a bedside lamp there was no electric socket for it and in any event with a bit of stretching I

144

could reach, from the bed, the huge brass electric light switch which protruded like a shining golden boil from the wall adorned with its brown railway-waiting-room paint. The air in the bedroom was hot and stale, and so I tried to open the sash window even though that would mean letting in the murk stagnating behind the retaining wall, but the sash cords were broken. To add to my exasperation I was quite unable to turn the rusted wheel to cut off the central heating, and I cursed the enormous ancient radiator and kicked the flanges of its dinosaurian flank, stubbing my toe. It just gurgled back at me.

When I suggested to the elderly maid, who was laying the table in our sitting room, that she delay serving dinner until the other doctor joined me, she told me that he was in bed, and often retired early because he found he needed a lot of sleep in our climate. After a lonely dinner, an even more elderly maid bustled in, cleared the table, stoked up the already roaring coal fire, replaced the huge child-proof fire guard, which took up far too much space in that small cube of a room, showed me where the bulging coal-scuttle was, stymied my attempts at conversation and withdrew in a froufrou of crisp starched apron. It was as hot as the ash-room in a crematorium and since there was no radiator to attack, and since I didn't relish flushing live coals down the lavatory pan, I tried to open the sash window; this I managed to achieve as a result of a thorough hammering with the heavy iron poker I found in the grate, indicating to me that this was the first time the window had been opened this century. The mist had descended further and swirled into the room like a cool breeze in the tropical heat. I had become allergic to the massive five-foot-wide heavy metal fire-guard which I removed and dropped out of the window. Using the huge cumbersome fire tongs

145

which must have started life in a gargantuan blacksmith's forge I was now able to pluck off the top two layers of burning coals, and they joined the fireguard.

It occurred to me that the reason the doctors' quarters were at blast-furnace heat, could be either that it was felt necessary to support the local coal industry – no doubt the antiquated central heating system was coal-fired – or that it was my supposedly sleeping colleague's aversion to our climate; but his aversion certainly did not extend to young nurses as the regular rhythm of girlish noises from his bedroom indicated. Though we were stable-mates with adjacent bedrooms I hardly ever saw him because he was never up for breakfast and generally missed dinner, but he was very active during the night when I was trying to sleep. His hospital duties appeared to be very light and non-urgent and were mainly concerned with elderly chronically-ill men, while my duties were entirely obstetric and therefore involved urgent work and night calls. I once asked him if he would stand in for me for a few hours one afternoon so that I could do a little shopping, but he replied that he was very sorry but he did not serve other men's women. So I really was single-handed.

The antenatal wards on the ground floor were well run by two first-class sisters, and the first floor labour ward, in spite of looking like a cross between a third-world prison cell and a mediaeval torture chamber, was ably managed by a middle-aged, kind and motherly sister. Next to the labour ward was the postnatal or lying-in ward ruled by a very large battleship of a woman with a black moustache, iron-grey hair and a thick neck set on massive shoulders. This revolting person dealt with patients and nurses in a severe and autocratic manner as though she were a warden in Alcatraz, and in fact her ideas of looking after mothers and babies would have been considered out of date even in the latter half of the nineteenth century. When I caught her actually boiling split sheep's heads in a cauldron on the gas stove in the ward kitchen, I was told that this was necessary in order for her to make poultices for women on her ward unfortunate enough to have milk-engorged breasts. In my disbelief I couldn't help repeating, with appropriate actions, the lines I'd learnt at school when I took the part of one of the three witches in *Macbeth*, Act IV, Scene I, "Round about the cauldron go; In the poisoned entrails throw." But when I asked her jokingly when did she propose adding, "Eye of newt, and toe of frog, Wool of bat, and tongue of dog," to the hell-brew, she threw up her prize fighter's arms revealing the soaking wet patches of foul smelling sweat in her cavernous armpits. She said in a loud baritone voice which caused me to doubt her gender, "This is my ward and I'm in charge of everything here, doctor, and that includes the breasts and the bowels." As I protested that this was the obstetric equivalent of the sort of treatment Charles II received on his deathbed in 1685 when a red-hot poker was applied to his forehead and hot pigeons' dung to the soles of his feet, I suddenly realized that what the Medical Superintendent at my base hospital had told me about this place was not a leg-pull, but was true. He had told me that, in his youth, there were gynaecology beds next to the postnatal ward in this building, and cauterization of the neck of the womb was carried out, not with a delicate electric cautery, but with a red-hot poker. The operating theatre was on the same floor as the postnatal ward where open coal-fires were kept burning night and day. When the end of the poker was flaming red, it was handed to a hospital porter who ran the hundred yards along the corridor like an Olympic torch bearer as far as the theatre door where, as in a relay race, he handed it to the theatre porter who passed it to the junior nurse who passed it to the theatre sister who handed the red-hot poker to the gynaecologist who plunged it into the waiting neck of the womb. I could visualize this Amazon, who now confronted me, thrusting the flaming poker with a sadistic gleam in her eye into the hands of the terrified porter keyed-up for a flying start to his hundred-yard sprint.

Later that week, when speaking on the telephone to my Chief at the base hospital, I mentioned the intransigence of the postnatal ward sister, and he told me that he had tried to get rid of her on more than one occasion but had failed, because her husband, a communist trade-union activist, was a very vocal, powerful, bully-boy member of the local hospital management team. She and her husband lived in a part of the next valley known as 'Little Moscow'. My Chief advised me to have as little to do with her as possible, and admitted that he kept away from her ward on his infrequent visits to the hospital. Acting on his advice I arranged my postnatal ward rounds when she was off-duty and, no doubt, plotting with her husband in Little Moscow. I also had a word with the Hospital Matron who was a dear, kind lady of the old school; she confirmed what my Chief had told me, and warned me that she was 'a dangerous woman' who'd made life such hell for many good nurses that they'd resigned.

After I'd been there a fortnight, I woke one morning and became aware of an unusual silence and a whitish light filtering in through the thin curtains of my cramped cell. There had been a heavy fall of snow, and the ugly valley had overnight become a chocolate box Christmas card. Work went on as usual and as the thermometer fell lower and lower, I began to be grateful that so much coal was being burnt to keep us all warm, but I noticed that as the days passed and the snow continued to fall, my colleague now spent most of his time in bed, and I was told that the snow was bad for his eyes.

In the antenatal ward I had a patient who was causing me concern. She was a stout woman in her mid-thirties who'd been married for many years, and though this was her first pregnancy she had not attended any antenatal clinics and had been admitted to hospital five days ago, at the request of her general practitioner. She had high blood pressure, swollen ankles and protein in the urine – a triad that indicates a diagnosis of pre-eclamptic toxaemia, which in its severe form can kill the baby *in utero* and permanently damage, or even kill, the mother. She was not due to give birth for another five weeks, and as happens in such cases, the foetus was stunted in growth. In spite of the strict regimen of treatment imposed, her blood pressure climbed alarmingly, the swelling spread to her hands and face, her swollen eyelids reducing her eyes to slits, and the urinary protein increased making her a candidate for delivery by Caesarean operation.

I telephoned my Chief who told me to get her to the base hospital straight away, so I ordered the ambulance, informed the patient and, after sedating her for the twelve-mile journey, asked for her husband to be informed. It was three quarters of an hour later that ambulance control rang me to say that the ambulance had failed, even with chains on the wheels, to get up the steep hospital drive because it was 'a sheet of ice'. I had not been outside the maternity block, where I lived at the top of the drive, for three or four days, so decided to check the position for myself and ended up flat on my back. The ward sister sent for me because the patient was now complaining for the first time of severe headache, with flashes of light before the eyes, light-headedness and pains in the chest. These symptoms, together with a new sign that became

149

apparent on examination of the back of the eyes with an ophthalmoscope, indicated that the patient was on the verge of having an eclamptic fit, one of the most serious complications of pregnancy which can cause the death of mother and baby. There was only one thing for it – an urgent Caesarean operation.

I telephoned the base hospital again and spoke to my Chief who agreed, but his answer to my enquiry of how soon he could get up here to carry out the operation left me dumbfounded:

"How the hell d'you expect me to get up there if the ambulance can't? You'll have to do the operation yourself, and God help you – the last Caesar done up there was eighteen years ago and mother and baby died."

It was useless for me to protest that I'd never done a Caesarean operation before, but had only assisted, and here there wouldn't even be an assistant – I might as well be in the jungle – he'd already put the phone down. The cold fear that followed did not last long. After all I had assisted at many Caesars, and anyway what was the difference? Only that I'd be wielding the scalpel myself – but without assistants. Instead of the usual two assistant house surgeons plus a paediatric doctor to receive the newborn baby, I'd have none. I also knew from the textbooks that a Caesar under local anaesthesia was the correct procedure in this case, but this form of anaesthesia was used in very, very few hospitals and I'd never seen it done. So I had to get an anaesthetist. There were none up here of course, so that meant summoning one from the base hospital – what if the anaesthetist on call had heard about the ambulance? There was only one way to find out. It was my friend the Indian anaesthetist who was on call – yes! he'd be here in an hour. I still feel guilty I didn't warn him about the ice, and still wonder if I did him an injustice in assuming he might not have come had he known. The knowledge that I'd have another doctor in theatre with me, even though he wasn't a scalpel-wielder, gave me some confidence and I told the patient and her husband of the change of plan. The husband had arrived on foot and obviously didn't know about the ambulance failure. I told him that the only chance for the baby was an immediate operation and since his wife's condition was worsening hourly, and had now become life-threatening, her best chance was urgent termination of pregnancy by Caesarean operation, and that meant operating here and now on the premises. The husband, a hefty no-nonsense sort of chap who was at least twenty years older than me, squared up to me and fixed me with a penetrating look.

"We've been trying for a baby for sixteen years and I want the very best for my wife," he said.

I did not flinch, nor consider it prudent to remind him that his wife's perilous condition was the result of her not having bothered to attend any antenatal clinics.

In normal circumstances the next steps were routine – summon the obstetric team, the paediatric team, order blood to be cross-matched for possible transfusion, inform theatre staff and check the patient's pre-anaesthetic medication. However, apart from my anaesthetist, I was virtually completely alone; the obstetric team consisted of myself, the paediatric team consisted of myself, and the hospital had no blood bank. My own blood froze when I discovered that the theatre staff for this major blood-letting operation was composed, not of the usual senior and junior sisters and two staff nurses, together with other trained nurses and an assortment of nurses in training, but of one sister who had not even seen an abdomen opened for forty years, and one very elderly hospital porter to act as a runner – maybe in his youth he had been the Olympic torch-bearer here.

It was not until then I learnt that for many years the theatre had been used only very occasionally, and then only for very minor eye surgery, carried out under local anaesthesia. The message I received from the distant central blood bank that blood for possible transfusion might be available tomorrow morning, depending on weather conditions and transport arrangements, was just the sort of news I needed, and highlighted the lack of co-operation from outside the hospital that I had come to expect during the last few hours.

I had already informed the Matron of what was going on and as a result she was in a highly excitable state. The words poured out, "This will put my hospital on the map and show the whole of the valley that we can cope with major surgery here and needn't send our patients down to that other hospital; I'll come to theatre myself." She then regaled me with a blood-curdling story of a Caesarean operation performed by a long-dead surgeon in the London hospital where she had trained as a young girl, emphasizing the drama – "Mother and baby fighting for their lives, blood everywhere." Knowing how very bloody a Caesarean operation could be, I managed to get away from her before she succeeded in destroying my last vestige of confidence.

Despondently I climbed the stone steps to the operating theatre. There I found the late-middle-aged sister boiling up all the ancient surgical instruments she had managed to find. They had been hidden away in the two huge Victorian mahogany chests of drawers standing, like Gog and Magog, one either side of the theatre door which, incidentally, opened directly onto the public corridor. When I expressed concern that anyone, including visitors, might wander into the theatre during the operation, she told me the door would be guarded by two burly hospital porters who, in their spare time, were public house bouncers. Cheerfully

152

she informed me that she had also sent for a screen so that the patient would not see the frightening array of instruments while waiting to be anaesthetized; I thanked her for her sensitivity. The theatre itself was a small square room with some tattered brown rugs scattered across the stone floor and a most attractive, large, cut-glass chandelier shedding light and coal dust on the operating table which had managed to creak its way through from the nineteenth century. As I made my way back to my quarters, I saw that the whole maternity block had become a beehive of feverish activity, with nurses and porters criss-crossing the corridors, and I remembered the Matron's words and her pride in her hospital. Quite suddenly I realized that, far from remaining aloof, I too had now become part of this old hospital whose staff were giving of their very best. This was *their* hospital and they were going to prove their loyalty in this, the most serious emergency the vast majority of them had ever experienced.

By contrast, the doctors' residence was as silent as the snow-shrouded churchyard in the valley below – apart from the occasional girlish squeals from my colleague's bedroom. I stood looking out of the sitting room window across the white roofs in the valley to the snow-covered mountain beyond as I waited anxiously for the anaesthetist. At last his car started climbing up the drive and I was quietly cursing the ambulance people who had failed us when, at the second hairpin bend, as if in slow motion, I saw his car start to slide on the ice, backwards and sideways off the drive, roll gently onto its side and continue sliding down in the snow until it came to rest, nearside uppermost, against a naked oak. I admit that my first thought, as I slid and tumbled down to his assistance, was not for him and his possible injuries, but whether he would be fit enough to give an anaesthetic. He was quite disorientated, crawling around inside the car trying to get out through the windscreen. I climbed up onto the side of the car and tried to open the front door, but I had not realized how heavy a car door is when one is trying to manipulate it at such a great mechanical disadvantage. I found I had to exert all my strength to open it and hold it open for him to climb out. At least he could stand, and his right arm was uninjured because, with his innate courtesy, he shook my hand and enquired after my health.

It was after I had helped him to the sitting room and put him to sit in the one easy chair, that I realized he was in a state of delayed shock. He became uncharacteristically voluble, his lips were blue and, as I often joked with him afterwards, he was the first Indian I'd ever seen go pale. I sent for tea, highly sweetened, and let him have a few sips, insisting he lay down on my bed until I considered he had recovered sufficiently to give a general anaesthetic, but then a dreadful thought crept slowly into my mind. All general anaesthetics are administered using a Boyle's anaesthetic machine, and I couldn't recall seeing one in theatre. I dared not let him overhear me enquiring about such an essential piece of equipment, so I left him and telephoned the theatre sister from the nearest ward; with dismay I heard her say, "What is a Boyle's machine?" Without even asking, I knew there would be none of the other essentials for a safe general anaesthetic – a laryngoscope, intubation tubes, suction apparatus and all the other equipment anaesthetists used. I hoped he would not relapse into secondary shock when I summoned up enough courage to give him the dreadful news; this was on a par with a surgeon being told there were no scalpels but he could be provided with a kitchen knife and fork to open the abdomen. When he had recovered as much as I thought he would that afternoon, I led him back to the sitting room and very gently broke the shameful news.

No one, to my knowledge, had ever heard him swear, but now he banged the table repeatedly to emphasize his round oaths, and must have disturbed my Pakistani colleague at his work, for he put his head enquiringly round the door and was told, in a torrent of abuse, to get out and stay out. I heard him retreat hurriedly into his bedroom and relock his door. When I felt that the ambience had cooled as much as it would, I took the anaesthetist to meet the patient and heard his sharp intake of breath when he saw how grossly obese she was, which would of course make his work even more hazardous. She could not be wheeled, even part of the way, to the operating theatre because there were no wheeled stretcher trolleys and, since there was no lift, she had to be carried on a canvas stretcher by six hefty porters, wheezing audibly as they negotiated the unforgiving stone stairs to the theatre. Somehow she was manhandled onto the operating table, which had been moved from its central position under the decorative chandelier to the makeshift anaesthetic zone which had been screened off from the operating area. I saw the anaesthetist wince as he picked up the antique facemask of the type used during the nineteenth century. It was merely a metal frame over which gauze had been stretched, and this he placed over the patient's nose and mouth to receive the drops of anaesthetic agent he dripped onto it, in the hope that she would go to sleep. This was exactly the same sort of apparatus and method used in Queen Victoria's last two confinements, and was known as anaesthesia 'à la reine', but now known derogatively as 'the rag and bottle method', oxygen being given from a cylinder via a tube held under the mask. This was anaesthesia as it was practised over a hundred years previously, and as I slipped behind the screen to scrub up I heard the anaesthetist cursing quietly about the staleness of the anaesthetic agents he'd been given.

Normally one scrubs up in a single downward jet of water, whose temperature is controlled using one's elbows to adjust the long horizontal levers of the taps to obtain an acceptable hot-cold mix of water. Here, there was only one huge square porcelain sink, known as a Belfast sink, with large brass taps which must have been over two feet apart, one delivering boiling water and the other ice-cold water. So the scrubbing up process involved rapid side-to-side rotatary movements of the body as one tried to avoid the pain of alternatively scalding one's hands and getting frost bite. The sink was fixed so low on the wall, that I found it easier to kneel as I swayed from side to side, and I heard the anaesthetist, who was also having a difficult time, say as he looked over the screen, that he would soon be joining me in prayer. The sister, after giving instructions to the bouncers at the door, joined me at the sink. She was extremely short and soon we were swaying from side to side in perfect unison, she on the balls of her feet like a broken-down ballet dancer trying to pirouette, and me on the tips of my kneecaps like an earnest evangelist eager to spread the Word. Each time I turned towards her as though in supplication, she swung away as though spurning me in a *pas de deux*. All we could see through the large plate-glass window facing us was the snow-covered mountain which rose so steeply that, even on my knees, I could not see the sky. After scrubbing for the prescribed number of minutes, sister, who had to take on the full-time duty of theatre sister, as well as try to act as my sole assistant, turned towards me and I saw her frightened eyes over her mask as she said, "I suppose it'll be all right if we keep our heads!" That was the last thing I wanted to hear, and as I turned my face upwards towards the white mountain in silent prayer, it started to snow again.

I was brought back to reality by the urgent voice of the anaesthetist, "If you want a live baby you'd better stop dancing around – she's blue and I'm having a hell of a job keeping her under – she's so fat, she's had double doses of everything." Gowned, gloved, booted, capped and masked, I had the operating table moved to the centre of the theatre, foot-pumped it up to operating level and ordered the head end to be lowered, but was informed the tipping mechanism had jammed. Meanwhile, sister had taken up her position facing me on the opposite side of the table, but she was so short that the patient's heaving abdomen was at the same height as her own wheezing chest, so for her the operating field was at mantelpiece level. A bouncer was summoned and instructed to remove and upturn the deepest drawer from Magog, and position it for sister to mount in order that she might have a clear view of the field of play. After sterilizing the skin of the burgeoning abdomen and towelling-up so that only the incisional area was exposed, I took the scalpel and in one downward sweep cut down to the muscle layer through skin and thick blubber from umbilicus to pubis. Blood welled up and brimmed over the edges of the incision and had already soaked the white towelling before sister had managed to find, and hand me, even one of the Spencer-Wells forceps which are used to clip the bleeding points after swabbing away the blood. This procedure was even more difficult because, instead of operating in a calm, stationary field, the belly was moving around like a ship on the high seas as a result of the anaesthetist's troubles.

Just at that moment the door opened and a smiling tubby man in a filthy boiler suit clumped into the operating theatre like a friendly teddy bear, and in a cheerful high-pitched voice said to the bravely battling anaesthetist, "Your car is on its side and the engine is running. Shall I turn it off?" I interpreted the raucous howls from the anaesthetist's throat as, "Yes, get out, you blithering idiot!" and the teddy bear was gone.

The bleeding controlled with rows of Spencer-Wells forceps on either side of the incision, the next step was to tie off each bleeding point with absorbable catgut, and remove the forceps to give a clear field in order to enter the abdomen uncluttered by metal. "Tie," I said, expecting sister to hand me about nine inches of catgut, position one of the forceps so I could tie the bleeding point, then unclip and remove the forceps, and cut the long catgut ends – the whole procedure taking a few seconds. What she did was to hand me an unopened glass phial containing five feet of catgut. "Open it," I said. Instead of using a phial-breaker to open the phial cleanly, she placed it on her instrument table, hit it with one of her heavy prehistoric instruments shattering the glass and, in extracting the catgut, cut her finger through her rubber glove. As I was wrestling with five feet of catgut, she went hunting for a dressing for her bleeding finger and another pair of rubber gloves. The near panic that had assailed me ten minutes ago, now gave way to a tremendous effort to control my temper and get that poor baby out pronto, urged on by the anaesthetist who by now had realized that he was not the only one in dire straits.

Knowing that any help from my assistant would only hinder me, I strove to do everything single-handed, and relegated to sister the simple duties usually given to a medical student seeing one of his first operations. I even helped myself to the instruments I needed, by stretching across the patient's pitching belly to reach sister's table and disentangle what I wanted from the heap of instruments one normally finds only in museums of medical history. At last I was able to enter the abdomen and, using a fresh scalpel, I made a transverse four-inch incision in the lower segment of the uterus, plunged my right hand into the womb under the baby's head, rotated it in order to deliver the face into the incision and, after swabbing the mouth and nose, gently flexed my hand inside the womb in order to deliver the head. Then, using my left hand to exert pressure on the top of the uterus, the baby boy's body slid like a warm white fish into my arms. He was pale and limp and I laid him head down across his mother's thighs. After identifying and clamping the bleeding edges of the uterus, I instructed the anaesthetist to give the mother an intravenous injection to help to contain the bleeding. Using a thin rubber tube I sucked the mucus out of the baby's throat; after further resuscitation and division of the umbilical cord he gasped and, thank God, started breathing spontaneously. He became pink within three minutes of delivery and cried when five minutes old and that cry, in the tense atmosphere of that theatre, almost brought tears to my eyes.

It did however bring forth an answering high-pitched sound that could only be described as a bark. It was a bark! Looking up towards the door for the first time since teddy bear had lumbered out, I saw Matron beaming at me wearing her full dress uniform with First World War medals, her frilled starched cap tied round her neck with a gigantic white bow, but wearing no mask. A high stiff white collar seemed to prevent her from moving her head, as looking straight at me she said, "Quiet, Fifi!" Glancing down I was horrified to see a small, neatly trimmed black poodle wagging what remained of its tail and looking up at me wide-eyed. What could I say? From near panic to near loss of temper to near tears of relief in such a short space of

159

time and now this! I wanted to laugh out loud at the absurdity of the situation and at the same time shout for the filthy animal to be removed from the scene of a major operation; the result of these conflicting emotions being that I said nothing. Apparently Matron had been watching everything from behind the screen, but was unable to contain herself when, after quarter of a century as Matron, she heard the cry of the first baby to be successfully delivered by Caesarean operation in her hospital, and had moved into the operating area followed by her poodle. The excitement was over and, after removing the afterbirth and membranes, I began the tedious task of suturing the incisions, and closed up after a swab and instrument count. The whole afternoon had been fraught with difficulties and this operation which, a year later and in normal circumstances, took me twenty minutes to perform, had taken one and a half hours.

Despite everything, the mother was alive, the baby was alive. I was mentally and physically drained, and so I think was the anaesthetist, because when the bouncers allowed the unwashed teddy bear to plod back into theatre to hand the anaesthetist his ignition key, he was greeted with a weak smile and a whispered 'thank you'.

There was no way out. The mother and newborn baby were taken to a side room in the lying-in ward and given into the care of the sheep-head sister who, as Matron had told me, had no experience of post-operative nursing. Very tactfully and diplomatically using noddy terms, I outlined to sheep-head the principles of post-operative care and, knowing she could hear but was not listening, I wrote it all down in simple language and as I did so the horns started sprouting out of her thick skull. The next day I was relieved to find my instructions were being carried out and that mother and baby were recovering well, but the old ram had gone home as soon as I had left the ward yesterday and had taken a day-off today, so the ward was being run by a competent staff nurse. As I did my ward rounds and clinics that day I could sense the almost tangible air of celebration in the old hospital, no doubt orchestrated by Matron, and I had a faint inkling of how a returning hero must feel.

However, this did not last as the next day on my morning ward round, I found my patient slumped flat on her back and wheezing, her sheets dirty and bloodstained with her head hanging over the edge of the unmade bed. There were bits of orange peel and uneaten food strewn over the floor of her overheated room and a roaring coal fire smoked in the grate. Her listless, disinterested demeanour was reflected in her glazed eyes, and her apparent indifference to my questions was understandable in the presence of that sinister ram of a sister, whose horns grew more menacing as she stood glowering on the other side of the bed. Instinctively I knew my patient was destined for the morgue within a few days if she remained in the clutches of this evil woman who was blatantly ignoring my instructions. There and then I knew what I must do. After examining the patient I informed that treacherous sister that I was going to order a chest X-ray, whereupon she told me that the X-ray department was closed because it was Sunday. My response was simply to instruct her to have the patient in the X-ray department in one hour's time.

I left the ward to consult with Matron who gave my plan her whole-hearted approval, and came with me to open up the X-ray department, which was on the ground floor next to one of the antenatal wards. We neither of us knew how to work the huge machine, but that would not affect my plan, and so when the six puffing porters arrived carrying the patient I directed them to place her on the X-ray table and dismissed them, as I did not want them to witness what was about to happen. As soon as they left I started to pull the most important looking levers and depress some easily accessible switches. Suddenly there was a blinding blue flash and the lights went out. While I reassured the patient, Matron produced a torch from her voluminous pockets and opened the door onto the corridor, which was also without light, but as arranged, she chaperoned me while I examined the patient and declared that she was now too ill to face the hazardous journey back up the stairs by stretcher to the lying-in ward. Matron then carried out the next stage of the plan by informing the sister of the antenatal ward, where I knew there was an empty side room, that she now had a new patient to look after. So far, so good, but the whole hospital was now without electricity, so I must have pulled some very important levers. It would be completely dark in a few hours and though to find one's way around by candlelight and flickering firelight would have its romantic side, it would hardly make for efficiency in a hospital setting. So I asked the telephonist to send for the hospital electrician on call who, instead of reporting to find out what he had to do, telephoned back to tell me that he did not work on Sundays. When I told him that the hospital was without electricity and asked him to arrange for one of his colleagues to attend to the trouble, he stated that he would see to it that no member of his trade union would answer my call.

It was Matron who divined the reason for this gross insubordination. The fellow I had spoken to was none other than the red-hot communist trade-union member of the local hospital management team and, worse than that, was the husband of the horned sister, who no doubt had filled him in about the new young doctor at the hospital when she went home to Little Moscow.

What was to be done? The antenatal sister looking after our celebrated patient had a brainwave. On perusing the patient's notes she had noticed that the husband was a self-employed electrician, and so just as he was about to leave after visiting his wife and baby, I asked him if he would do me a favour. The hospital electricity was restored within ten minutes. He said he was only too glad to be able to be of some service to the hospital that had saved his wife and baby. He could never know the true story.

Sometimes I wonder what became of that baby boy – now, I trust, a middle-aged man – who made history as 'The Snow Caesar'.

THE RING

Your ring glittered in the sunlight as we laid your wedding bouquet on my father's grave. But now the sun is paler, the skin thinner and the bones more brittle. Too late, I am fulfilling a promise I made to my confidant, Leopold Kohr, many years ago to write down this story from the beginning. Too late, because on the Ides of March 1994 Leopold was laid to earth in his birthplace, Oberndorf – the village of 'Silent Night' – while the whole Province of Salzburg mourned.

★   ★   ★

I had promised my patient I would perform her second planned Caesarean operation using exactly the same technique of local anaesthesia as I had used for her first Caesar, because again she wanted to hold her baby the very instant it left her womb. I had arranged to do the operation in ten days' time, and was actually passing through the hospital gates at the start of a few days' leave when I was called back – my patient had gone into premature labour – with the result that I only just made the night train out of Paddington.

After a nightmare journey I was dozing, half aware that the train was no longer running smoothly, but was racketing along on what appeared to be an uneven track, when a sudden jolt restored me to some sort of consciousness, and I fully expected to hear yet again the cruel, compelling call, 'All Change', echoing through the cold night air. But it was not so. Too early in the morning the empty train had juddered to a halt at my stop, and I tumbled out to find myself alone on the one-horse platform in the uncertain grey light of a bleak winter's morning, disappointed that no one had come to meet me.

★   ★   ★

As a result of reading an article in 1960 about the remote Welsh gold-mine which supplied the gold for the royal wedding rings, I had, unknown to my fiancée, written to the holder of the gold-mining licence. With the carefree arrogance of a young surgeon I had informed him I would be visiting the area in the near future in order to be taken to the mine to mine some gold. I received a telegram informing me the mine was closed. With the air of authority bred of a spell in the armed forces, I replied by telegram giving the date and time of my arrival at the nearest railway halt; and here I was, a young man trim in his (almost) Savile Row suit, black with a faint grey stripe, the bottom button of the waistcoat and one cuff button left undone, white Rotten Row mac thrown casually over the shoulders, and carrying calf-leather riding gloves. After taking a few turns on the apology for a platform, I was surprised to see a small, wiry octogenarian with a weather-beaten face set off with a white goatee, slowly emerging from behind the trunk of a large oak tree growing alongside the railway line, and my impression was that he had been sizing me up. He was wearing a thick, rough overcoat and advanced towards me quite quickly in spite of his age and a decided limp. As I told him of my cold, miserable journey he seemed singularly disinterested, and then I said I had not had any breakfast. His remedy was to take me to the village pub and, though it was only just over an hour after sunrise that gloomy, sunless morning, he rousted out the sleepy landlord and told him to draw two pints of bitter beer 'on the slate'.

Though not a pre-breakfast beer drinker I felt obliged to return his hospitality and, after I had lost count of the rounds, he produced from the inner recesses of his heavy, green coat a selection of hideous, ornate, Victorian gold jewellery – watch-chains, necklaces, brooches and tie-pins. These he arranged on the round grey-marble top of the small three-legged, iron Victorian table which held our wet breakfast. When he started offering to part with the various items, 'at bargain prices', I had to inform him I had not travelled hundreds of miles to buy pawnbroker's gold trinkets, but wanted Welsh gold from the mine for a wedding ring.

"Good boy, we'll drink to that! It must be very wet in the mine after all the rain we've had, but you're such a keen young man, I'll take you there."

I could have been mistaken, but I fancied a hint of a wink passed between him and the landlord.

With pints of beer slopping around in my stomach, which had been empty for the best part of the previous twenty four hours, we somehow managed to meander to a house where his middle-aged partner in the mine, taking the whole picture in at a glance, hurriedly left his breakfast, insisting that he, and not his hoary old partner, drove their battered old four-wheel-drive jalopy to the mine entrance. And what a spine-chilling ride! It was like being on the South Bank Big Dipper on the edge of a precipice going up the side of a tilting mountainside, with the added joy of experiencing wave after wave of nausea. Fortunately before my stomach finally rebelled, the old man and I were deposited at the barricaded mine entrance in the side of the watery mountain, our driver saying cheerfully he'd pick us up in four or five hours, in order for me to catch the train back to London. I did wonder why he was chuckling quietly to himself as he clasped my hand and wished me good luck.

167

After we had removed the barricades of steel bars, rusty iron bedsteads and rotting planks, the old man produced a number of keys and after much fumbling managed to open the several padlocks, and then with a huge iron key found the keyhole in the heavy metal door which didn't exactly swing open – it was as much as we could do to push it inwards far enough for us to squeeze inside. My enthusiasm for the venture was not enhanced when I discovered that it was a roof-fall of rock behind the door that had made it so difficult to open, but I desisted from asking when the door had last been opened, as I thought the answer might sap my confidence even further. By the light of his carbide lamp the old boy insisted on locking the door from the inside and with considerable difficulty slid some rusty bolts into position, 'in case strangers get in', and as he turned away and left me in partial darkness, I instinctively reached into an inside breast pocket of my suit, and yes! – my pen-torch was there. I put out my hand and found I was caressing a smooth slimy rock face. When the old man turned back I could see that he was now wearing a safety helmet. I had no safety helmet. A narrow passageway glinted in the lamplight between wet, black rock faces. Without a word he started shuffling forwards and I followed, but after a few dozen steps I heard the water sloshing around his Wellington boots and as I rolled my trousers up to my knees, I wished I hadn't worn my thin, black city shoes – but at least my black silk socks would soon dry out.

The roof was more uneven than the floor, as I found to my cost when my forehead hit a jagged piece of rock. Thereafter I ambled forward in a crouching position like a Neanderthal man, knees bent, arms outstretched in front of me, my white mac flapping against the black walls like the wings of a lame bird trying to fly in a freezing, wet tunnel; my only light was the reflection of

the yellow beam of his ancient lamp on the wet rock –
suddenly even that disappeared. He had turned a sharp
corner in the adit. I stopped, reached for my pen-torch
to discover that an instrument that gives excellent
illumination of a patient's throat was ill-suited for use
in the intestines of a mountain. I rounded the corner,
and in trying to catch up with the lamplight, I stumbled
and fell cutting my bare knees. Soon afterwards words
of blasphemy rang through the tunnels as my companion
plunged up to his waist in a water-hole. Though I tried
to negotiate the hole very gingerly on tiptoe, the icy
water lapping at my crotch made me yell out so loudly,
that the old man turned around and warned me that
any sudden, loud sound could bring the roof down.
Subdued, I crept along behind him almost on all fours
with my head twisted to the left as far as it would go in
order to try to see where I was going, since that was less
tiring than holding my head in hyperextension. It was
then I discovered I could see nothing with my right eye.
I felt around the eye; it was sticky and the pen-torch
showed blood on my fingers – a good demonstration of
why we have eyebrows, because by twisting my head to
the left the blood from the cut on the left side of my
forehead had run down between my eyebrows over the
bridge of my nose and ended up in my right eye. When
my cocked-up left eye told me the bobbing helmet
ahead had gone down more than a foot or so, it meant
the old man was crouching and, being much taller, I
was reduced to crawling on my bare hands and knees,
scraping them on the rock. It was the ease with which
he negotiated these frequent tube-like stretches that
made me wonder if he had dropped easily out of his
mother's womb and spent his formative years wriggling
in and out of dark passages. Whereas I, the product of
a difficult instrumental home delivery, was by now the
victim of incipient claustrophobia. It was not pleasant.

When I ventured to ask, "How much further?" I was told that he had thought I was 'really serious' and he had intended taking me to the best vein for tapping, but if I was just wasting his time I might as well get out of the mine now. I reassured him that I was serious. He grunted and forged ahead and I followed like a deformed ape through a maze of narrow slits in the rock, taking so many turnings to left and right into different tunnels that I was completely disorientated and knew I would never find my way out of this mine alone. After about another half-hour of mental torture, during which time I fought to control my mounting apprehension and prevent my mental state slipping out of control, he stopped. I was relieved to see that the passage was now wide enough for us to stand side by side, and I was able to look into his face for the first time since we entered the mine. But I was not standing alongside a benign old man with twinkling eyes. He had changed. He was grinning, showing his broken teeth, but his eyes were hooded and fish-like. A frightening thought fluttered in and out of my mind – perhaps he was dementing. I realized I was completely dependent upon him, lost in a labyrinth of tunnels. The yellow beam of his lamp seemed weaker – what if it failed? What if he had a stroke? He was very old and maybe wanted company to die inside the entrails of his beloved mountain. I heard the quavering echoes of my own disembodied voice asking, "Where's the gold?" though by now I didn't care – all I wanted was to get out alive. He didn't answer. He just lifted his right arm and pointed upwards and I was shocked to see he only had one finger growing out of his withered right hand. Why hadn't I, a medical man trained in observation, noticed this before? Was this the same old man who'd met me at the railway halt? I followed the direction of his twitching finger. It was pointing to what looked like an oversized rusty square bucket.

The lamp beam ranged slowly over the whole sinister contraption – the bucket, the rusty chain and the winch, and then I saw to my horror that we were standing only a few feet from the edge of a yawning black hole. As if to compound my fears, the light of the lamp moved slowly downwards into the hole which swallowed the beam in its black depths. With his left hand the being at my side turned the winch handle and to the harsh rasping of the worn-out chain links he lowered the clanging bucket and nodded for me to step into it. No one has described the sensations I must have experienced at that time better than Edgar Allan Poe in his story 'The Imp of the Perverse', where standing at the edge of the abyss his first impulse is to step back, but for that *very* reason he inexplicably and perversely takes the fatal step – forward. I can only assume that in my case, the Imp of the Perverse combined with an excess of early morning alcohol had blocked any rational thought processes. At that time I had not heard Leopold saying, 'When you stand at the brink of a precipice there is only one thing to do – step back.'

I took off my riding mac and handed it, with my gloves, to the grinning winch operator, and stepped into the bucket. As I started to descend he handed me a little hammer and I heard his cackle as he thanked me for the 'nice mac'. Just when my head was disappearing below the mouth of the hole, he told me to start chipping when the bucket stopped and to use my pen-torch. Was he still cackling or was that the sound of the corroded links of the chain grating unwillingly on the roller? I gripped that chain as firm as any drowning man grips his lifeline. The rim of the bucket reached only halfway up my thighs and, as it started to swing from side to side, I had to squeeze down onto my haunches or I'd have been tipped out into the unknown. I don't know how far I went down into that hellhole but as the lamplight became fainter and fainter, so my voice became feebler and feebler as I tried to sing my favourite funeral hymns. I consoled myself that at least they'd identify what was left of me from my wallet, but then didn't rats eat leather too? Here I was, a supposedly rational human being, albeit in an alcoholic haze, with everything to live for, swinging to and fro in simple harmonic motion, crouching in a bucket on the end of a disintegrating chain in almost complete darkness, my life dependent on the whim of a strange old toper, with only one functional hand to control my descent into a bottomless pit.

Like the clapper of a church bell that has run amok, my heart was striking the inside of my rib cage rapidly and violently as though it meant to crack it. To add to my claustrophobia and intimation of impending doom, I was finding it difficult to get my breath in the still, dead air. I was too far down in the vertical shaft to hear if the chain was still unwinding, but the increasing amplitude of the swing of the bucket from side to side meant I was probably still descending in that black void. Then gradually the sides of the bucket started scraping the walls of this devil's chimney, which had already stripped the skin off the back of my left hand. Like the last trumpet of doom a distant inhuman yowl echoed and re-echoed through my narrow prison and when the ululation had died away there was nothing – just nothing. Apart from the feel of the cold rock that enclosed me I was in a state of complete sensory deprivation, in total blackness with the eeriness of absolute silence about me. The bucket had stopped moving, and how long I remained cramped up in it before nervously standing up I cannot tell. But I had disturbed something in the menacing silence of that awesome place. From somewhere down there came a muffled rustling noise, then a faint leathery sound as though the desiccated folds in the skin of an embalmed mummy were being prised apart; but when a draught of air, like the last breath of the dying, swept up past my face I shuddered at the thought that I was easy prey encoffined in my vertical tomb; at least Ben Jonson had the protection of a proper coffin when they buried him standing upright.

At last I remembered my pen-torch and by its beam saw that my square bucket was hard up against solid rock on two sides, but down between the other sides and the rock face the abyss plunged down. Gripping the pen-torch between my teeth and holding on to the rusty chain with one hand, I threw down a large piece of rock I'd found in the bottom of the bucket. I counted the seconds before I heard the long drawn out boom of the splash reverberating ominously up and down the shaft, and calculated that I was suspended about one hundred feet above deep water. It must have been the sloshing of the angry waves heaving up against the walls of rock in the deeps below, and echoing in the rock-tube, together with all the beer I'd drunk, that gave me an overpowering desire to pee. Slowly I turned away from what might be waiting down there and surveyed the rock face, which on two sides was no more than a foot from my own face. There was indeed a thin reddish-yellow vein in the rock running from eye level on the right to armpit level on the left.

Thinking that the bucket would now be unlikely to tip, I let go the chain and took out my pocket-handkerchief which I held under my little hammer as I chipped away at the vein. Though I did not expect gold nuggets to leap out at me, I was disappointed that my

173

efforts resulted only in some moist grey grit on my white handkerchief and unfortunately in my eyes as well, but the fact that I was actually doing something helped me to keep control of myself and I continued to chip away. It was very tiring work and during my frequent rest periods, when I switched off my torch to conserve the battery, there was nothing – no light, no sound – nothing, only the feel of the slimy rock, and the spectre of near-panic hovering close in the chill of the dank air. I was buried alive in my sepulchre, perhaps to be discovered in years to come and labelled, 'The Skeleton in the Bucket'. The only escape from the nightmare was to click on the narrow beam of light and to start chipping again. I was collecting more wet grit and had almost filled my handkerchief when, with the grating sound of metal on rock, the bucket began descending and within seconds was hurtling down the shaft, its iron sides clanging against the walls. I lost my balance; my head pounded against the rock; there was an unearthly shriek; a vivid intense whiteness.

Gradually the kaleidoscope of disordered words sorted themselves into, "He's come back." I was lying on the jagged rock floor of hell, a little hammer was hacking bits of bone from the inside of my skull, a searing light was scorching the inside of my eyeballs and I was choking on a throatful of whisky-flavoured blood. Clutching a small flask, he was bending over me, his pointed beard inches from my face, muttering about a 'blackout' and a 'chain slipping'. My only coherent thought was about the whereabouts of my precious handkerchief – yes it was there, tight in my left fist – and I lapsed back into the lap of unconsciousness. In my lucid intervals I heard the old man grumbling about his lost hammer, and I heard the echo of my own voice cursing him and his hammer. But as I turned my head to escape the torture of the light, I glimpsed at eye-level a square of dented rusty metal like the side of an ancient dilapidated tank, and in my returning consciousness, became aware that he had winched me up out of death's maw, and something told me to stop swearing at him. As though an observer, I watched the painful process of my body rolling onto its belly and slowly getting onto its feet and, to my amazement, saw my arm encircle the old man's shoulders, but in retrospect I don't know whether this was in gratitude for saving my life, or in order to steady myself.

My memory of the journey out of the bowels of that grim mountain is a hell-brew of uncontrollable trembling, of falling, of hands and legs sticky with blood, inflamed eyes full of grit, forehead cold with sweat and a blur of light drifting around in an endless maze. The hammering inside my skull had become a dull regular thudding and now was more insistent, but when it became irregular I ran through the list of causes of irregularity of the pulse in a young person and, as I'd been taught at Guy's, chose first the most serious diagnosis in the hope of being able to exclude it, but I could not exclude it – and it was mortal. My disordered senses had led me to believe that the thudding was inside my skull, whereas it was in fact outside, and was reverberating through the tunnels of the mine. It was the old man's partner hammering on the mine door trying to break it down because we'd been in the mine nearly six hours, and as he told me later, the mine workings were extremely dangerous and lives had been lost. There had always been a strict no-alcohol rule in the mine and, furthermore, he recalled that his partner had recently suffered from blackouts, but since I was a medical man he thought everything would be all right! However he soon found out this had not been the case. The old man was mute; his face in the bright moonlight as pale as a leathery face can get. I was anything but mute and, after laboriously climbing into the relative comfort of the bone-shaking jalopy, I caught sight of my face in the driving mirror and was surprised at the contrast between the chalk-like pallor that showed between the dark clots of blood on my face and the vivid red of my blood-filled eyes. I reached into the pocket of my torn and filthy trousers and, like an excited schoolboy, produced a large wet bloodstained handkerchief tied at the corners and bulging with grey sludge. There was no comment. The hair-raising drive down to the house was no longer hair-raising and after transferring the precious contents of my handkerchief into a large jam jar, I cleaned up as best I could. Next I promptly vomited the bacon and eggs the younger partner had kindly cooked, whereupon the old man offered me a jugful of the home-brewed cyder he was drinking. This I politely declined and asked for a glass of water.

They were so mindful of my welfare that I thought it would be churlish on my part not to agree to accompany the younger partner to the nearby stream where, by the light of the moon augmented by a powerful torch, he demonstrated to me the art of panning, whereby the yellow gold could be separated from the gravel by agitation under a little water in a large shallow metal pan. We found no gold in the material he panned and I hoped he did not think me ungrateful for turning down his offer to pan the wet gravel in my jam jar. I didn't tell him that to my surgeon's eye it all looked remarkably primitive, and that I had visions of the bullion merchants in Hatton Garden vying with one another for the privilege of extracting the Welsh gold from the contents of my jam jar.

I can still see the game old man and his sensible, courteous partner standing under the lamplight waving goodbye, as the last train, hissing and hooting, pulled away into that wide but secret valley, the river shining cold and silver in a moonscape so breathtakingly beautiful. Though exhausted I was determined to stay awake to guard my treasured jam jar, whose coldness was balm to my burning, lacerated hands and I have to admit I attracted some curious glances. I must have presented the appearance of having recently been in a punch-up with my swollen eyelids, my red eyes, my cut and bruised face and hands, torn and dirty clothes and bloodstained shirt. In fact some nervous passengers left for other compartments, especially when they noticed how protective I was of my only bit of luggage – an oversized jam jar full of grey mud.

*　　*　　*

Back in hospital even my patients seemed wary of me, and I was conscious of the sidelong glances they exchanged with one another as I passed from bed to bed during my ward rounds. Neither was I *persona grata* with my surgical colleagues because for about ten days my torn hands precluded me from 'scrubbing-up' to operate, which meant they had to deal with any surgical emergencies, though I was able to postpone non-emergency operations until my hands had healed.

In the meantime I had discovered the whereabouts of the royal nugget of gold and my first afternoon off-duty found me in Hatton Garden. Carrying my jam jar I marched through the imposing portals into the even more impressive reception area of the headquarters of Johnson Matthey Ltd, Bullion Dealers, Gold Assayers to the Bank of England. I may have been mistaken, but I had the feeling that my most courteous reception was tinged with a certain apprehension and I was informed that a member of the assay department would 'look into my problem'. He proved to be an affable, well educated young man from New Zealand and was a good listener.

"I'll get the contents of your jam jar analysed," he said. "I'll initiate a feasibility study in order to assess the possibility of extracting the gold and, if there is in fact any present, I'll get it assayed for the purpose of fashioning a wedding ring."

He was such a decent chap I didn't even ask for a receipt, but said I would telephone in a fortnight's time and it was then he told me they had managed to extract the Welsh gold, but there wasn't enough to make a wedding ring, and asked for my permission to make up the deficiency with ordinary gold. When I protested, he suggested that instead of ordinary gold they could add some platinum to my Welsh gold in order to make the ring and I acquiesced – they already knew the size – and the ring would be ready in a week.

I owed so many emergency on-call duties and operating sessions to my colleagues, that a fortnight went by before I could take another half-day off-duty to go to Hatton Garden. The ring was beautiful and they'd even engraved the name of the mine on the inside. The administrative staff and the men who had extracted the gold and those who had fashioned the ring, were so intrigued by my story that there would be no charge; also permission had been granted for me to view the nugget of Welsh gold which came from the same mine, and which was used to create rings for the royal family. It was a very large nugget. But I never got my jam jar back.

★   ★   ★

It was many years later I discovered that my dear friend Leopold Kohr had laboured manually, not for one day for but six weeks, in a gold-mine in North America, after he had been forced to flee his native Austria for repeatedly denouncing Hitler at the Anschluss. Forty-three years later the Government of the Province of Salzburg awarded him its highest honour – the Golden Ring. Among the many national and international awards he received for his humanitarian work, the one he cherished most was that Golden Ring. Maybe it was these parallels, tenuous as they are, that prompted Leopold to make me promise to write all this down, but now it's too late – or is it?

WHO THEN WAS CREMATED?

There was just time for the routine shower, but no lunch, after my morning's operating session, because one sticky case had been particularly bloody and I'd sweated more than usual in that hothouse of an operating theatre. The service of thanksgiving for the life of the surgeon I'd returned to replace, after many years' absence, was due to begin in twenty-five minutes, and I should have known the hospital chapel would be full to overflowing because he'd been so popular.

He'd always taken pride in his appearance, both with and without his clothes, and the memory of my first meeting with him so very long ago came back vividly to me in the shower. I'd applied to be his house surgeon and had been called for interview. The hospital secretary told me that the Chief wanted to see me before the interview and, taking me along endless corridors past doors bearing various surgeons' names, we arrived at an operating theatre suite.

"In there," he said smiling knowingly and, shouting my name out, pointed to the door labelled 'surgeon's changing room'. He'd had to shout to be heard above the fruity baritone voice singing one of the bluer rugby songs.

I went in for my pre-interview interview and there he was – the surgeon who wanted a houseman – a fine figure of a man standing stark naked dripping after his shower. "Come on in, boy," he said extending his hand, "I've sent the student nurse for some coffee – pretty little thing she is too. Tell me how much cutting have you managed to get under your belt? You'll get plenty here."

In answer to some timid knocking on the door he trumpeted, "Come, my dear," whereupon a lovely young girl, in a tantalizingly skimpy theatre gown tied loosely behind, brought in a tray of coffee and ginger biscuits. As she bent over in front of me to place it carefully on a low table, he winked at me as he followed my gaze and continued, "Oh yes, you'll spend a lot of your time in theatre here, but they're a friendly bunch and you'll have plenty of opportunity for social intercourse."

Blushing, the girl whispered, "Thank you, sir," and, as she turned to leave, her gown billowed out and I fancied there was a subtle hint of a delicate girlish fragrance.

Yes, he'd been a fine figure of a man.

As the most recent addition to the consulting staff at the hospital, a seat in the third or fourth row from the front would have suited me, but it was standing room only and still ten minutes to go. However, my old friend who'd been Matron of the hospital when I'd been a junior doctor here so many years ago, had kept the seat next to her for me. She was one of that now long-dead breed of hospital matrons who had commanded the respect and affection of doctors, nurses and ancillary staff alike, and she had come out of retirement to pay her last respects to a fine surgeon who'd suffered such a horrible death.

The hospital secretary who, with two clerks, still ran the whole business side of this large hospital ushered me to my seat, and I wondered if he remembered how he and I had won the cup for doubles tennis so very long ago.

Matron and I were sitting directly behind the widow and children in black. I really should have skipped that shower and got here before them. The Matron (I'll always call her that) now looked small and frail and, as she took my hand, I saw that her kind blue eyes still glinted keen as a friendly scalpel. She was as dignified as she'd been, all those years ago, when in my wild young days, she'd had to speak to two of us house surgeons for indiscretions involving two of her nurses at a hospital dance – no one else could have done this with such salutary effect. Nowadays it would be done by a specially convened disciplinary committee of five managing pen-pushers and politically acceptable members, who'd turn pale at the sight of warm blood welling up in a wound. The hospital scenario now is non-medical employer and medical employee, though maybe there'd be input from a doctor and nurse who'd found hospital work too demanding and had become subordinate managers. But I digress.

I wanted to chat to Matron so much, but even my whispered voice echoed in that silence. Furtively I glanced at my pocket watch – only two minutes before the tension would be relieved by the stainless voice of the hospital chaplain. The stifling heat emphasized the sickly sweet scent of flowers.

Suddenly there was a commotion at the back of the chapel. Voices were raised and it sounded as though someone had fallen. There was a rustling of best clothes and service leaflets as the congregation turned to look behind. Matron and I, made of sterner stuff, continued to face front and I remembered the warrant officer's words when I was in school, 'If a bomb explodes behind you when you're on parade you don't move – not even your eyes', and no doubt Matron had had similar training. But the rustlings and sharp intakes of breath swept up behind us like waves, and now there was a muted cry, followed by a thud as if a heavy body had slumped to the floor. Still I didn't turn around – I was a surgeon, wasn't I! There were plenty of physicians sitting behind me to see to it – a fit of the vapours was more in their line, wasn't it? It seemed as though someone or something was staggering down the aisle behind us, limping and dragging one foot, bearing down upon us very slowly, but insistently – a footfall, a pause and then a long slithering sound, another pause and what sounded like a gasp followed by another footfall.

The suspense was too much – Matron turned towards me to look over her shoulder. I have seen many go into sudden shock – the pale grey, moist face with a hint of cyanosis about the lips, and have heard the shallow breathing – but I had never seen it happen as quickly as it did with Matron that afternoon. As I put my arm out to steady her I looked up. There, nodding and grinning down at me, with a set of false teeth too large for his mouth, was the skull-head of the man whose houseman I had been so long ago, and whose place I had now taken. His shell was bending over me, the thongs of his neck twisted ropes coming up out of the collar which was far too big, the smart navy blue suit draped loosely on what must be a skeletal body hung with drooping flesh. But the dancing blue eyes, the high forehead and the quiff of hair were unmistakable.

Before I knew it, I was on my feet, and this time it was me that extended my hand. He took it but said nothing. It was not a handshake. My hand was trapped, entangled in the claw-like clutch of a mass of finger bones. But the clasp was as firm and assertive as it always had been. This was the hand of a brilliant surgeon, the hand of a man who had been taken fully conscious with a presumptive diagnosis of black malignant smallpox to die in the lonely smallpox hospital on top of the mountain. After the awful obsequies prescribed to prevent the virulent infection spreading from the corpse, a body had left in a sealed polythene bag inside a closed airtight coffin packed with sawdust saturated with carbolic acid. The hearse with police motorcycle outriders and flashing headlights had sped to the crematorium twelve miles away. Who then had been in the coffin? I knew that the frightful appearance of the face of the corpse of someone who had died of black malignant smallpox might well render it unrecognisable. Who had been burnt in the oven at the crematorium that dreadful day? He'd always been a great leg-puller – was this his last trick? Perhaps that's why he was grinning. He let go my hand, lurched forward and slumped into a seat. But his widow, head bowed, did not seem to be aware of the hideous, nodding death's-head alongside her.

The young padre, who'd never met him, commenced the service of thanksgiving, but his voice resounded round the walls of a half-empty chapel. He paid eloquent tribute in his best ecclesiastical voice to this man he'd never seen, while the subject of his eulogy sitting right in front of me, shifted uneasily. During one of the prayers, an order of service leaflet was passed to Matron who passed it on to me. The pencilled note on the back implied that the ghost of my old Chief sitting in front of us was his identical twin, who'd had a stroke and was entering the terminal stages of a fatal wasting disease. No one in the congregation, apart from the widow and children, had known of his existence.

THE ELEVENTH COMMANDMENT

It was the second time I'd seen a policeman faint. The first was at a road accident where a drunk in a fast car had driven head-on into a bus and had been decapitated. I found his head in a field, but unlike the case of King Charles I, no one bothered to stitch it back on. Incidentally the vicar told me later that the beer fumes emanating from the coffin during the funeral service made the chancel smell like a public bar.

The second time it happened was when some blood-soaked dressings had to be removed from the neck of a man who'd botched his attempt to commit suicide by slitting his throat at his house in the early hours of the morning. He been stitched up in the operating theatre, but had started bleeding again from a small vein just under the suture line, which stretched from ear to ear. After attending to this minor hiccup I found the policeman crumpled up on the floor of the single-bedded hospital room. He had insisted, against my advice, on remaining in the room, because his superior officer had instructed him to keep a close eye on the patient, who had allegedly murdered his wife about twelve hours ago. Her throat had been cut so deeply with a slaughterman's knife, that the hack marks on the front of the vertebral bones at the back of the neck could be seen in the depths of the gaping wound, once the blood had stopped gushing out. Hence the police presence, as the patient was being detained for questioning on a criminal charge.

The Medical Superintendent, a distinguished surgeon who was head of the hospital, in the days when hospitals were run by doctors for the benefit of patients, had asked the heads of the major clinical specialities for our help. He wanted us to provide junior doctors to oversee the care of this patient, on a two-hourly day and night rota. One of my six doctors had refused on religious grounds, so I had volunteered to take his place, and was given the ghastly details.

It appeared that the couple lived in the same street as a police station, and but for the immediate response of the police, alerted by the neighbours who had been woken by the shrieking of his wife as she was being murdered, he might well have succeeded in his suicide attempt. She was found lying across the bed, the walls of the room dripping with her warm blood, which had spurted out of the depths of the yawning gash in her neck from the severed carotid arteries, like water gushing from a burst water main, as she had run helplessly around the bedroom, like a half-decapitated chicken, trying to escape from the murderer's knife. Her husband, a slaughterman by trade, was found standing in front of the blood-spattered wardrobe mirror, having made several tentative cuts through the skin of his neck just under the left ear, trying to pluck up courage to make the deep slash and slit his throat properly. After the crash of the front door being broken down, he had heard running footsteps up the stairs, and had seen in the red-smeared mirror two policemen bursting into the death chamber. At that moment, he drew his slaughter-man's knife purposefully across his neck and slumped to the floor, but he had failed to kill himself as he had not severed either his carotid arteries or his jugular veins. As so often happens in this method of attempted suicide the head is thrown right back to clear a path for the knife, and this action draws the carotid arteries and jugular veins backwards out of harm's way, behind the thick muscles in the front of the neck, so that the air passages and voice box bear the brunt. This man, besides cutting through a great deal of neck tissue, had in fact sliced through his Adam's apple and had he not been brought to hospital so very quickly would have choked to death by inhaling his own blood.

The casualty medical officer had immediately performed a life-saving operation by cutting into the air passage below the Adam's apple to insert a curved metal tube down into the windpipe. Using a suction apparatus he sucked the blood and mucus out, thus creating a clear airway, before calling in the duty surgeon who repaired the severed tissues. On either side where it entered the neck the metal tube had winged flanges with tapes attached and it was fixed in position with a few sutures, and further stabilized by tying the tapes behind at the nape of the neck.

The post-operative care can be onerous. A rota of trained nurses was drawn up by the Matron, so that there was a nurse with the patient throughout the night and day. The nurse had instructions to call the duty doctor if there was any change in the man's condition and, in any event, the doctor on rota duty visited frequently during the two hours he was on call. On my recommendation any policeman on duty remained in the corridor outside the room, and looked through the observation porthole in the door as often as he wanted.

The man was nursed sitting up, in a well-ventilated room maintained at seventy degrees Fahrenheit, and the head of the bed was protected by a canopy, while humidifiers prevented the air becoming too dry. Feeding was by intravenous drip and the usual nursing care was given for the bodily functions. Oxygen and carbon dioxide were at hand in case the patient stopped breathing, which could easily happen if the level of carbon dioxide in his blood dropped too low. Beside the bed was a trolley containing various instruments for emergency use, if the need arose. The breathing of a patient in this condition should be inaudible, but in this man the respirations were bubbly, and mucopurulent matter had to be sucked out of the trachea using a rubber catheter and syringe – not a very pleasant procedure for the doctor on duty. Neither was it a pleasant duty for the nurse to wipe away the offensive secretions he coughed up, in order to prevent him sucking them back in.

However, in spite of being given prophylactic antibiotic cover, the wound became infected and broke down, so debridement with insertion of rubber drains had to be performed under general anaesthesia. He then developed bronchopneumonia which is a frequent and usually lethal complication in such cases. It was only by dint of intensive medical and nursing care over a period of two weeks that he survived long enough for the gaping wounds in his neck to be resutured. About this time an attempt was made to half-cork the neck-tube to encourage more normal breathing, and during the fourth week the tube was removed completely, after he had been able to breathe normally for five consecutive nights with the tube fully corked during sleep.

He had been unable to speak for some weeks because of the damage he had inflicted on his own voice box but his voice gradually returned, though weak and husky, and he was able to indicate answers to police questions before being discharged into their custody. This was nearly six weeks after his admission to hospital. Altogether over thirty hard-pressed junior doctors had, in addition to their normal duties, overseen his post-operative care day and night, on a completely voluntary basis; quite apart from the three consultant doctors involved. Although we had saved his life, I was not alone in calling to mind, on more than one occasion, the doctor's eleventh commandment, 'Thou shalt not kill but thou shalt not strive officiously to keep alive'. At the trial that followed some months later he was convicted of murdering his wife. He was hanged by the neck until he was dead.

THE VAULT

He had been standing behind me in the vestry for the past hour, and each time I turned a page of the mouldy old church register I felt his hot breath on my neck as he peered over my shoulder, and I could hear the ruffling as he slid his hand into his inside breast pocket to take out his biro, and make yet another mark in his little book when my search entered another year. He was a pale, spotty young curate with halitosis; the nape of his neck was a pink bed of angry yellow-headed boils. I felt vaguely uncomfortable in his presence.

This was during my genealogical period when, spurning mere copies in libraries and record offices, I spent much of my spare time haunting churches looking through the original centuries-old registers of baptisms, marriages and burials; sometimes freezing cold in a church vestry by the light of an oil lamp in the small hours of the morning with mice scuffling in the wainscot; sometimes warm and welcome with tea and cakes at the dining room table in a vicarage. I knew there was a standard fee payable per year searched, but during many years of searching the registers I had not been monitored before, nor asked to pay, and in any event I invariably trebled the due fee in my contribution to the church funds.

Spelling just did not seem to matter until the end of the eighteenth century, and I was engrossed deciphering the meaning of the words in the faded script before me with the aid of a magnifying glass, when I became aware of a whispered conversation, and on turning in my seat saw that the curate had moved to the door of the vestry and was pointing towards one of the chapels in the church, giving directions to a cheerful-looking middle-aged man wearing a stonemason's leather apron. The directions were apparently not clear enough, because the curate told me I must leave the vestry in order that he might accompany the stonemason to the chapel that bore the name of an illustrious family. Whether the curate thought I might take a peek at a few more years without paying, or grab the whole register and make off I don't know, but he locked the vestry door after me.

It seemed that a member of this ancient family had recently been placed in a vault under the floor of that particular chapel, and the heir to the title had told the stonemason to position the engraved stone plaque in the chapel as nearly directly above the body as possible. The curate was of no help, so the stonemason said he would have to enter the vault to check the position of the fresh coffin, and with my help proceeded to roll up the carpet runner in the aisle, while the curate stood back wringing his small, soft, white hands. We came upon a wooden trap door in the slate floor and on raising it found a heavy metal manhole cover, which we levered up, releasing an updraught of cold air with a peculiarly sweet though musty smell. I don't know why I had expected to find stone steps but there were none, and kneeling on the cold slabs while the curate looked on in distaste, we were unable to see into the depths of the hole in the chapel floor.

In an outbuilding that was used to store the bier and the gravedigger's spades, the stonemason found a ladder and he and I lowered it slowly into the yawning darkness. It seemed a long time before it touched bottom, and it had to be positioned practically vertically in order that one could ease oneself through the small hole. The curate demurred when the stonemason invited him to accompany us down the ladder – I had already volunteered. We were just about to descend when we realized we had no light, and to protestations of incredulity from the frothing curate, we grabbed a huge altar candle each. The stonemason went down first and, with my foot on a rung of the ladder, I asked the curate, who stood trembling in the gloom of the chapel, if he did not consider it his duty, since this was a vicarless parish, to come down with us into the vault, but I received no reply. As I disappeared down the hole I caught sight of his white face, his eyes wide, his mouth wider, and heard his sharp intake of breath as I disappeared from view. It seemed a long way down and when I joined the stonemason at the bottom of the ladder, I saw by the flickering yellow light of our candles that we were standing in a wide passage with plenty of headroom.

As I followed the stonemason along the passageway towards the sanctum underneath the altar where he thought the corpse might lie, our measured footfalls seemed deadened; they were the sombre beats of a muffled drum warning us that we were about to trespass in a very private place. But I was quite unprepared for what happened. There was a sudden unearthly howl as my companion disappeared and his candle was extinguished. Involuntarily I jerked my arms upwards and my own tall candle hit the ceiling, flew out of my grasp and went out, spilling hot wax on my hand. In the total blackness I heard groans coming from somewhere down below, and I admit that I had the frightening feeling that we, as strangers, were being threatened in some way by a ghoulish malevolence for violating the peace of this centuries-old family vault. I dropped to my knees and groped around on the floor and found my candle, but then realized I had no means of relighting it. I crept forward on all fours, the candle between my teeth. The groaning was now coming from behind me and I realized that in the utter darkness I had become disorientated, and was crawling away from the stonemason – if indeed it was him that was groaning. Turning, I inched very slowly towards the disembodied sounds. The floor of the passage became slippery and I tried not to think where the mucoid-like matter on my hands might have come from, as I neared the mournful sounds below. Sliding my hands forward in the slime I found that the floor ended abruptly, and I was kneeling on the edge of what I took to be a sort of pit. From below me came a voice, "Where's your bloody candle?" I replied I had no matches. Feeling around in the pitch dark I found that the edge was in fact the edge of a deep step, which I soon discovered was the first of a very steep flight of stone steps. Even though I climbed down backwards very carefully on all fours, my hands and feet were not able to maintain a hold in the slippery slime, and I slithered down the last two or three steps landing on my knees in some soggy matter alongside the stonemason.

After relighting my candle with his matches I discovered that my colleague could not move because, as a result of the fall, his foot had become jammed under him in a crevice in the stone floor which had long ago collapsed. After a painful extraction of the foot I found the second candle and examination by the guttering light of two altar candles showed that the foot was still functional. We got to our feet and in a few yards found ourselves among stalactites and stalagmites in a damp chamber, whose floor was slippery with sweet-smelling slush, and whose walls were honeycombed with deep slate niches, each able to accommodate a full-sized coffin. Indeed most of the niches were already occupied, some closed with a slate plaque bearing the ancient family name, title and dates and others open with the head of the coffin in full view. Ferreting underground by candlelight in the dank, fermenting air of a burial chamber, among a cache of stacked coffins, some with the leather cladding still intact, some disintegrating, was a macabre experience. In the spluttering, pale yellow light I caught an occasional ghastly glimpse of a piece of greyish white shroud. Had the sad locks of silk-like auburn hair and the delicate eggshell fingernails, shimmering for a moment in the guttering candlelight, really been that long when the vault was sealed?

At last we found a freshly polished ebony coffin in the far corner with the head protruding a foot or so from its niche. At this point the stonemason informed me that the deceased had been "one of those tall aristocrats". However, he said he had to be absolutely certain that this was indeed the correct corpse, and he asked me if I had any objection to helping him pull the coffin out sufficiently for him to read the nameplate. Though I had represented the Home Office in a supervisory capacity at some highly unpleasant exhumations, this was different. Intuitively I felt I would be tampering with something best left alone, and I hesitated. But when I saw the candlelight glinting on the silver coffin-plate smile spreading knowingly across my companion's face, I of course agreed to his request. It took all our strength to pull the heavy coffin out a few feet to reveal the nameplate of the eleventh viscount, but the unmistakable sloshing sound as we pushed it back too forcibly into its resting place sickened me.

At the far end of the vault, a flight of stone steps led up to a huge stone slab which closed the churchyard entrance to the vault, and with a slight break in his voice the stonemason informed me that this stone slab would probably never be moved again, since the present holder of the title had married a Semite and both had compromised and embraced the Roman faith. After noting the measurements needed to position the plaque in the chapel above, we began our return journey, and negotiating the treacherous floor and the slimy steps, arrived back at the foot of the ladder without mishap. We were just about to climb out of the passageway when we both heard a sound, something between a sob and a whimper, which seemed to be coming from a low narrow tunnel we hadn't previously noticed. We decided to investigate, and tiptoed quietly, bent double, in single file along the uninviting tunnel, candles held low. Negotiating a bend we saw a faint glimmer of light, and deciding to take the intruder by surprise we extinguished one candle; after our previous experience we crept forward extremely carefully, snuffing out the second candle only when we were able to see our way by the light ahead. In complete silence we stood at the narrow entrance to a claustrophobic chamber. Two closed coffins and two opened coffins lay on the stone floor among scattered pieces of dismembered coffins whose contents were strewn around. It was a gruesome but pitiful sight.

Standing in the centre of the sepulchre with its back to us was a figure holding an oil lamp and dressed in what appeared to be a long black coat; it seemed to be staring down intently at one of the coffins. Very quietly we crept into the crypt and as the stonemason brought his hand down on the intruder's shoulder, he let out a piercing shriek and dropped the oil lamp as he crossed himself. It was the curate. We relit our candles and he told us that he had decided it was his duty to check what we were doing, but had taken the wrong turning, ending up in this vault. It appeared that he had been transfixed by what he had seen in one of the coffins when we surprised him. Its lid lay upside down on the floor and its lead lining seemed to have burst open, spewing out some of its contents. He was in a highly nervous state, and in an effort to calm him down by showing him something of interest, I picked up an adult male thigh bone and holding it against my own thigh, demonstrated that the owner had been taller than I was. I then persuaded him to hold it against his own thigh hoping to get him used to handling the ancient bones, but unfortunately a sharp spicule of bone penetrated the skin of his index finger drawing a little blood. He made an unholy fuss about this tiny wound and in order to divert his attention from it, I picked up a normal adult skull and a huge translucent hydrocephalic skull from the same coffin, and to show how paper-thin the hydrocephalic skull was, I placed a lighted altar candle inside it. The curate became distraught and freaked out at the grotesque sight and grabbing the other altar candle, turned and fled.

We were not impressed by his behaviour, especially as he had taken our one box of matches, which he had borrowed in a fruitless attempt to relight his oil lamp. So we were left with one lighted candle, a shattered oil lamp and no matches. Undeterred we continued our investigations in the bone chamber. One of the two intact coffins was large and was still sheathed in thick opulent leather, bound to the underlying outer wooden shell by domed brass studs, some of which still glimmered gold in the candlelight. The nameplate on the lid, inscribed three and a half centuries ago, bore the name, title and coat of arms of a family extinct for over two hundred and fifty years. Wedged between the crypt wall and that coffin, as though for protection, was the small coffin of a child, but the nameplate was missing. While I stood in that crypt gazing sadly at the small coffin, and wondering if modern medicine could have saved this child, who might well have been the last of that noble line, the stonemason jerked me back to reality by handing me a small skull and pointing to a hole in its roof said, "It must have been a violent death." It was the skull of a baby and the hole was in fact natural – it was the anterior fontanelle which normally closes between the ages of one and two years. I was fascinated by the variety and ages of the bones, and calculated that the skeletal remains scattered on the floor represented the bodies of four adults, one child and one baby. But most harrowing of all was to see the few tresses of fair hair tied with ribbon, which crumbled in my hands. The fact that there were no rings on the fingers nor any jewellery among the confusion of bones that still lay inside the broken coffins, nor among the bones, bits of lead and coffinwood scattered over the floor, indicated grave robbers. But why had the subhumans that had perpetrated this desecration spared two of the coffins? These, and other thoughts were churning in my mind, and as I ran my fingers over the smooth callus that had formed at the site of a fracture in an ancient arm bone, there was a sudden crash, then a clanging noise which reverberated through the passages followed by a rush of air and our only candle went out.

Would a man of the cloth do such a dastardly thing? Neither of us had told anyone where we were going that winter's afternoon. Was this a repetition of what might have happened centuries ago, and were there really more skeletons than coffins? Shakespeare's epitaph flashed before me – "Curst be he that moves my bones." Was this retribution for what I had done in this charnel house? Would someone centuries hence find another two extra skeletons in what was now our prison? As though reading one another's thoughts we both broke into stilted laughter at the unspoken absurdities. In turning to put the arm bone back in the coffin I tripped on the uneven floor and fell forward full length into the open coffin, to the ghastly sounds of brittle bones snapping and eggshell skulls cracking under my sacrilegious weight. I rolled over the edge of the coffin onto the floor before getting up, to try and avoid any further insult to those unhappy remains and, spitting out a few bone fragments, I stood up. My friend, for surely he had now become that, was laughing at my clumsiness, but he must have been made of sterner stuff because I had an overwhelming feeling of shame and remorse for what I had done.

We felt our way around the powdery walls of that chamber of skeletons, unable to find our way out, and I thanked God I was not there alone. We were completely disorientated in the inky blackness and the only companions we had down there seemed somehow to have become menacing, and I had the uncanny feeling that I was being threatened. I told myself this was absurd, but once the clasp on the lid of the subconscious has been released, unwelcome thoughts can escape and swirl up into the conscious mind. Our nervousness increased and as I hit my head on a low ceiling, I lost my balance and with my back to the wall I involuntarily thrust out my arms to break my fall. But my hands struck another wall and I realized I was no longer in the bone crypt, but at the mouth of the low narrow passage, and I cried out in relief to my friend who must have been still circling the sepulchre. He begged me to keep talking so that he could home in on my voice, but it seemed a long time before he caught up with me. Very slowly we crept forward, bent double now and still in complete darkness, until suddenly we both tripped and fell over the ladder which was lying on the floor, my friend injuring his wrist. There was no light from the chapel above and no words were needed to describe the seriousness of our situation, but I applauded my comrade's choice of words, "The pimply bastard!"

With great difficulty we managed to lift the ladder and by drawing its end back and forth across the ceiling eventually found the position of the manhole and, with as much power as we could muster, pushed the ladder upwards to try to lift the heavy metal cover from below. After very many attempts over a period of about twenty minutes we managed to shift it, and to our surprise the ladder shot upwards through the wooden trap door and a glorious grey light shone down on us from either side of the carpet runner which had been rolled back into place but was now impaled on the end of the ladder. Thanking God and cursing the curate we scrambled up and out of that place of the dead, and after dragging the ladder up and replacing the manhole cover and trap door, we went in search of our mutual friend. We found him giving instructions about flower arrangements to a little white-haired lady.

Having already decided on his punishment, we waited until he'd run out of flower-talk, and when the dear lady was leaving by the West door, he attempted to follow her but found his way barred. We took him back to the vestry and while the stonemason kept him in custody, I went into the village and bought a gallon tin of concentrated agricultural disinfectant with a particularly evil smell that clings to the body and clothes for a long time. I also bought a scrubbing brush. Using cold water from the churchyard tap I filled two buckets with a strong solution of the foul stuff. We told the curate that the denizens of the vault had probably died in agony from the plague, and we were very worried that he might have become infected from the sharp shard of bone that had drawn blood from his finger. To minimise the risk to himself he should scrub himself all over using every drop of the solution in the two buckets, and let it dry on his skin and not wash nor use a towel for four days – all a pack of lies of course. He stripped completely and did as we told him behind locked doors in the vestry. While bending down over one of the buckets, he accidentally kicked over the three-quarters-full gallon tin so that all the concentrated, stinking contents poured out, soaking his clothes, which were in a heap on the floor, and all the surrounding carpet.

When the stonemason and I took our leave, the stench in the vestry was overpowering and the curate himself smelt like a polecat on heat. While we were stowing the ladder away in the gravedigger's shed, we noticed two elderly ladies who were about to buttonhole the curate in the churchyard, suddenly turn and hurry away, lace handkerchieves to their delicate noses.

When I met my friend the stonemason a few months later, he told me that soon after our little adventure the vestry had been fumigated and a new carpet laid. The curate was obviously unable to divulge what had happened without incriminating himself, and had been transferred to an appointment where he had no direct contact with members of the public.

Thirty-three years later I visited that part of the country again. The stonemason lay in the churchyard. The chapel had been converted into a hall by partitioning it off from the rest of the church, and children in white shorts were playing badminton, innocent of what was just underneath. A wooden stage had been erected over the chapel entrance to the vault, but I managed to crawl underneath the stage and find the wooden trap door. When I lifted it up, the metal lid of the manhole had been concreted over.

SMALLPOX ON HOLIDAY

If you'd been unfortunate enough to catch fulminating smallpox you'd be doing everyone a favour if you insisted on them keeping well away from you as it's highly infectious and invariably fatal. You would remind your doctor, as tactfully as possible, of his statutory duty to report to the Medical Officer of Health (nowadays called the Consultant in Communicable Diseases) who bears the ultimate responsibility for the complete control of the whole complex situation, whether in hospital or in the community. Although you'd be only too aware of your rapidly approaching end, you'd be fully conscious right up to the moment of death and would be well advised to choose your undertaker as you'd need his services within a few days. However, he might not be too keen to handle your offensive corpse and would probably suggest a rival firm, which anyway would stipulate a quick cremation before you'd be really cold because the smallpox virus doesn't like cold dead bodies, and would metaphorically jump at the chance of being transferred to the warm living body of the undertaker.

But don't worry unduly, the public health doctors have succeeded in ridding the world of smallpox, and the World Health Organisation actually said so in 1980 and preventive vaccination against smallpox has been discontinued. However the possibility now exists that a psychopathic dictator, bent on world domination, might gain access to the smallpox viruses still kept alive in a few high security locations and wreak devastation across the world.

At the time when this universally fatal fulminating

smallpox was still around, I happened to be working at the epicentre of one of the most serious visitations of this Angel of Death in the twentieth century. John Bright's words that we could 'almost hear the beating of his wings' were apt as there'd already been many funerals of the unvaccinated, but nearly all of us at the hospital had been vaccinated and assured that as a result we were now protected and would be most unlikely to catch it. But the general public knew that people who worked in my hospital, though not ill themselves, could still act as passive intermediaries or 'carriers', bringing the smallpox virus out of the hospital on their clothing or in their throats, so you didn't get too close to hospital workers in case you accidentally brushed against them, or they coughed at you. I saw many a café, shop and bus empty very quickly if a hospital worker entered, and many pretty nurses were deserted by their boyfriends, though fortunately after a few months people began to forget and things returned to normal.

That then is the backdrop, and now the stage is set for the performance which took place four years later and a hundred miles away.

It was a glorious summer's afternoon when, as the Medical Officer of Health, I received an urgent telephone call from a local doctor who had been called to see a schoolgirl on holiday in the seaside resort where he practised. He thought she might have smallpox, and she had not been vaccinated. Rather unwisely he had told her parents of his suspicion, and naturally they were very upset and wanted to share their worries by telephoning their relatives in the large city where they lived. Knowing only too well from experience it would only be a matter of a few hours before the gutter press and the mass media were broadcasting all manner of false and sensational information, causing panic among the townspeople and holidaymakers – I'd seen it all before – I immediately telephoned the parents and managed to persuade them to keep these suspicions to themselves, at least for twenty-four hours.

There had been no smallpox outbreaks in this country for the last four years and the history I obtained from the girl's parents was quite unlike that of smallpox. It would have taken me over two hours to get the complete garb required to deal with a case of suspected smallpox and it would most certainly have upset the girl to be examined by someone dressed like a member of the SAS. In view of these facts I decided to take a calculated risk and, after taking her own history, I examined her wearing rubber gloves and a simple mask.

She was certainly quite ill and her rash was not chickenpox which is the commonest disease to be confused with smallpox. The type and distribution of the rash fitted in with a diagnosis of smallpox, but she had not been ill for long enough and was not now as ill as I thought she should have been if she in fact had smallpox. My colleague was not convinced, and since I knew the manifestations of smallpox could be protean, I decided to call on the National Smallpox Panel, which consisted of the very few doctors who had seen literally hundreds of cases of smallpox abroad, and were now resident in Great Britain. This I did, and it was arranged that an ex-Indian army doctor who, incidentally, had been a Major-General and now lived near Birmingham, would be called out of retirement to give his opinion. I was assured that he had seen thousands of cases of smallpox in foreign countries where it had been endemic. We made the girl comfortable and informed the parents of the position and, after arranging to meet the retired Major-General the next afternoon at 3 o'clock, went our separate ways. But my way was anything but smooth.

It was a beautiful summer's evening. The little town was heaving with happy holidaymakers wandering around barefoot in beachwear, eating ice cream and chips, and if one half closed one's eyes one could imagine the sea was actually blue. One word from the girl's parents and this would change overnight. There would be an invasion of newspapermen licking their pencils, television crews with their intrusive cameras and radio interviewers with all their paraphernalia. All this would lead to a mass exodus of frightened holidaymakers to their homes in so many different parts of Great Britain that, if this were indeed smallpox, contact-tracing for protective vaccination would be so time-consuming as to be too late to be effective. I recalled the recent 'polio incident' with the wholly unnecessary scaremongering induced by the media, and how I'd been obliged to spend a great deal of my time attempting, without much success, to counter it, and I remembered also my annoyance and frustration at having to deal with the irresponsibility of many of those in responsible positions in the media. Ah well! It might never happen – the parents seemed quite sensible people.

It was getting late and too far to travel back to my main office, so I let myself into a satellite office I had in this small town and telephoned my wife to say I'd be late home, mentioning I'd just seen an interesting case, 'query smallpox'.

"OK, thanks for letting me know. See you in three-quarters of an hour and don't be late. By the way, your mother turned up this afternoon so there's something special for dinner."

"Pull the other one," I said.

"Honest, she's here, so you can stop pulling my leg too."

"I'm not pulling your leg. I have just seen a case of 'query smallpox'."

I thought the line had gone dead; then my wife said slowly, quietly and in measured tones, "What did you say?"

"Yes it's true, but not a word to anyone – remember the polio. I've got an old ex-Indian army buffer coming to have a shufti tomorrow."

Then in a very determined voice my wife said, "Well in that case you're not coming home here. You know full well Mary hasn't been vaccinated. You'll just have to stay in an hotel."

It had been considered too dangerous to vaccinate our six-year-old daughter Mary, when she was a baby, because she'd had eczema and vaccination in those circumstances can be fatal. So she was completely unprotected and of course my wife was correct. Why hadn't I remembered?

"OK, I'll ring when I get fixed up."

All the decent hotels were bulging with visitors but eventually I managed to book a room in a rather run-down hotel about twenty miles away. Dinners were over but – "Yes, we'll do you a sandwich." When I rang home later from my local office it was my mother who answered the 'phone. I told her to think of me nibbling at my stale cheese and pickle sandwich in the seedy hotel where I was going to spend the night, while she was enjoying an elegant dinner with my wife and daughter at home.

Like a bullet her voice shot down the telephone wires: "What on earth d'you think you're doing putting all those people at risk in that hotel! Don't you know anything?"

Although I knew the chances of my acting as a carrier of the disease were remote – very remote – I could see the headlines, '*MOH Causes Smallpox Epidemic.*

MPs Demand Public Enquiry'. What could I do? Would the Aussies still hold it against me that I'd turned down a consultancy in Melbourne some years ago? I rang the hotel and cancelled the sandwich and bed. Now what! Though it was now early evening the shops were still open taking money from the happy holidaymakers clogging the pavements, but as a result of those two 'phone calls home my imagination ran riot. I found myself walking in the gutter to avoid accidentally brushing against one of these carefree people, some wearing nothing but bathing trunks, innocent of the fact that the man who looked so out of place in his suit and tie could be the harbinger of a terrible death if he touched them. I thought of the poor lepers of old in their cowls ringing their bells to warn people to get out of the way, and of those oblique slits in church walls – leper squints – allowing lepers to take part in the services without actually entering and contaminating the church. Realizing that it was much easier to catch smallpox than leprosy I moved out of the gutter into the road and got sworn at by an irate motorist in a large yellow Ford. I was hungry and thirsty but since I couldn't now enter a restaurant or café I made for the fish and chip take-away, only to find a long queue, which of course I couldn't possibly join because people in queues jostle and brush up against one another. Maybe if I waited a bit the queue would disappear, so I went to sit on a bench and looked at the sea which had by now become its usual grey, boring self.

"Hello, doc, enjoying the ozone?" and with that an affable, bandy-legged little man sat down right beside me. Though I had no idea who he was, I certainly didn't want to give him smallpox, so moving quickly away to the other end of the bench and turning my face away from him, I got up saying the first thing that came into my head, "I've got to make an urgent 'phone call."

As I walked quickly away hoping he wouldn't follow, I heard his muttered exclamation which sounded like, "Oh, not good enough, huh!" It was as I was walking along the seafront five minutes later that I remembered having seen him before. He was a local councillor who, unknown to himself, had caused me so much trouble, and as I laughed out loud and long at the memory of what had happened, a respectable looking couple, out for an evening stroll, looked askance at me and made a grab for their two young children.

It must have been eighteen months ago when I'd been asked to give a talk on brucellosis, which was causing concern in the county, that I'd met that councillor. After I'd finished my half-hour talk and answered numerous questions from the very appreciative audience of farmers and local representatives of the public, this little man came up to me as I was leaving the hall and said, "Tell me doc, what is this brucellosis?"

Instead of saying as I would if I'd been talking to a class of schoolchildren, "Have you been asleep for the last half-hour?" I just made a throwaway remark as I was in a hurry to get to another meeting and said, "It's something like Tb, but I'd rather have Tb than brucellosis."

It was some weeks later that a friend sent me a cutting from a local newspaper. The headline was, 'MOH would rather have VD than Brucellosis'.

During my aimless ambling around the bustling seaside town I was approached by two people I could only vaguely place, and a nod sufficed for them, but then the headmaster of the local secondary school came up to me. He'd telephoned my secretary the previous week to ask if I would give a talk to his sixth-formers on the history of preventive medicine, and he obviously wanted to discuss the date and time with me. But as soon as he stopped to talk, I dodged past him and broke into a trot saying I was in a great hurry, and when I glanced back, he was standing still, watching me with his mouth open, shaking his head slowly from side to side. To avoid any further embarrassment I decided to drive into the country.

It was an evening to remember. The sky was a cloudless azure, the setting sun scarlet as it slowly dipped below the edge of the sea, but I had to turn my back on all that as I drove inland in search of my own company, and this I soon found as a result of taking unsignposted side roads. Soon I was utterly lost and pulled into a small lay-by to assess the situation. It was dusk as I left the car and sauntered slowly up the narrow road which eventually became a track with grass growing in the middle, but I must have needed even more solitude because I left the track for a footpath which led me into an oak wood. Before long I found myself sitting on the grass in a clearing, leaning against the trunk of a giant oak tree and watching the stars appearing one by one like sparks burning holes in the black umbrella of the night sky. For a while there was no sound at all and I became aware of the regular rhythm of my own breathing, but before long there was a gentle rustling in the undergrowth at the edge of the clearing, as if whatever lived there had now accepted that this intruder could be ignored for the time being. I don't know how long I'd been sitting there, but it was by now quite cold, the leaves shivering in a fresh breeze, the clearing bare in the cool feeble moonlight and somewhere in the distance, deep in the velvet shadows, I heard the bark of a fox followed by the hooting of tawny owls – maybe that's what woke me up, or was it that I felt quite chilled? The light from the eggshell moon, now just clear of the trees, outlined the edges of the clearing and it crossed my mind that if I were discovered, clad in suit and tie, in the sudden beam of a powerful electric torch as I sat there under the cold glitter of the myriad stars, explanation would not come easy. I couldn't tell the truth, so what could I say in answer to the perfectly reasonable question, 'What are you doing here?' To answer, 'I am a poet in contemplation, attendant upon the Muse' would sound dubious. I'd better get up and try and find my way back to my car – at least there are heaters in it.

There was enough light to cross the clearing and find the beginning of the path that led between the trees, but soon the branches, heavy with leaves, blocked out the faint light from above and I was reduced to shuffling along with my arms outstretched. Suddenly my head was jolted back by a painful jab under my right eye. I had lumbered into the unyielding, broken end of a branch at eye level – a black eye for sure, and more explanations. To avoid any further accidents I inched along the rest of that woodland path in a crouching position with one arm across my eyes and the other feeling the way like an outstretched proboscis. It took a long time to get out of that wood into the weak moonlight, and even then I lost my way and found myself among an inquisitive herd of cows who, one after the other, started following me. But when the leading animal – was it a bull? – began to trot and the rest of the herd took up the theme, the adrenalin started to flow; I became more athletic than I thought possible and my pupils must have dilated because I was able to see much better as I leapt over a five-bar gate to safety.

Eventually I found the car, flopped down in the driving seat and switched on the heaters. Of course they just blew in cold air, so I had to drive around to warm up the engine and ended up hot and tired in a lay-by where there happened to be a telephone kiosk. I was just about to make a reassuring 'phone call home when

I caught sight of the car clock, and decided no one would be full of joy receiving a 'phone call in the early hours of the morning, so I might as well get some sleep. I took off my jacket, tie and shoes and curled up on the back seat. It was still dark when I woke up to the eerie shriek of a barn owl. I was shivering with cold so I climbed into the driving seat and revved up the engine to get warm. After a few minutes with the engine at full throttle, I noticed lights had been switched on, windows were being opened, babies were crying and angry people were shouting and gesticulating at their opened windows. I had not realized there were some houses on the road directly opposite where I had parked, so I quickly drove off and found a friendly disused farm gateway, where I pulled up and settled down again on the back seat, but this time wrapped in a filthy oily blanket I had remembered was in the car boot.

It was not the frightening shriek of the barn owl nor the comforting call of the tawny owl that woke me. It was probably one small bird that cried out when it woke with indigestion and started up a chorus of sympathy from its fellows, resulting in an increasing cacophony of searing high-pitched cries of annoyance, from larger and larger birds with more and more capacious, resonant voice boxes. At least that was my interpretation of the dawn chorus that morning. This sadistic trait is often found in humans too – 'if I can't sleep, then I'll make sure you can't either'. Was this what made me look through the car window for the telephone box in order to ring home? I didn't do so for two reasons and I hope the first was the true reason. It would be uncharitable because it was not yet six o'clock in the morning and unlike the loud-beaked creatures that had woken me up I was not uncharitable, and secondly there was no telephone box there anyway; and

212

it was then I remembered why. When I uncurled myself from the foetal position I'd endured during my few hours of uneasy sleep, I became aware of stiffness and aching in joints and muscles that I, a trained anatomist, had forgotten existed. I was chilled and thirsty and the inside of my mouth tasted and felt like the fur on the belly of a plague-bearing black rat, and one look in the driving mirror confirmed that the beefy red swelling around my right eye was now taking on a purple hue.

I got out of the car and, like a primitive being, went in search of water. Five fields later I found a sluggish stream and managed to scoop enough stone-cold water into the palm of my hand to rinse out my mouth and discover all my amalgam fillings. While I was thus engaged on creaking knees, to all appearances in early morning worship of the pagan god of water, I was hailed by a cheery voice, "Morning doctor, you're up early, trouble with the wife? Lovely day isn't it." Too late I realised that my "Yes" to this farm-worker's statement about the weather, also embraced an affirmative to his question about my domestic affairs, but knowing how some minds work I knew that to add a denial in answer to his cheeky question would only lead him to believe the opposite, so I merely smiled sickly and he lumbered off nodding his large head. I couldn't recall having met him but assumed I must have treated his wife or children at some time. Still cold but aching less, I went back to the car and drove around the brightening countryside for an hour or so, with the heater and radio on, and was relieved there was no mention of smallpox on the news. By about eight o'clock I returned to the lay-by I'd been obliged to leave in a hurry some hours previously and deemed it an appropriate time to telephone home and make some sort of plans. My wife and I arranged that she would bring me some clean clothes and my sponge bag

213

so that I could brush my teeth and shave, and she would meet me at a quarter to nine at a road junction a few hundred yards from our house.

Opposite the telephone kiosk was a small shop which had already opened and while buying potato crisps and lemonade and exchanging civilities, I was regaled with a blow-by-blow account of how some inconsiderate fool – probably a visiting yobbo in a stolen car from an inner city – had woken up the neighbourhood in the early hours of the morning by revving up his car engine, but had driven off at such speed that no one had managed to note the registration number of the car. After agreeing wholeheartedly that "someone ought to put a stop to this sort of thing", I drove off quietly so as not to arouse suspicion and pulled up some miles away to enjoy my breakfast of crisps and pop. In spite of having been awake for hours, I only just managed to make our meeting place in time.

The timing and meeting place could not have been chosen any better to make the maximum impact upon the neighbourhood. My wife was already there, having just deposited our children at the school across the road, and it seemed that the mothers of all the children for miles around were bringing their offspring to school at that very time. I drew up alongside my wife standing at the roadside, but she immediately retreated a good five yards from where I stood and proceeded to throw towels and various articles of clothing at me. My trousers landed on the bonnet of the car, but I managed to catch a parcel containing socks and underclothes, and although I caught one shoe, the other landed on the road and was retrieved by a lady taking her little boy to school, and I still remember the look of sympathy she gave me as she handed me the shoe and asked if my black eye was painful. Meanwhile my own children and other pupils were looking over the schoolyard wall at the domestic drama being enacted right in front of them. Each time I advanced a little closer to my wife in order to catch an airborne article, she retreated and was heard to say, "Keep away from me."

But that was not all. Who should be passing on a tractor but the cheerful farm-worker I'd met earlier, who grinned knowingly as he waved to the parents he knew. My tattered sponge bag was just about to follow in the aerial arc described by my clothes when, realising it would break open scattering my toilet requisites all over the road, I shouted, "No, just put it on the road and I'll pick it up."

My wife did that, and as I advanced to pick it up she retreated, so that the curious parent-audience which had now gathered were treated to our elegant *pas de deux*, my wife maintaining the same five-yard distance from me as I moved around. I was unwise enough to enquire after my mother to be told she would not have me anywhere near the house.

As though confirming their worst suspicions the assembled parents began nodding and muttering among themselves and I overheard phrases like:

". . . black eye."

". . . stands up for herself."

"They say it's the drink . . ."

"His mother knows him . . ."

". . . you can never tell."

But I was relieved to hear a different type of comment made no doubt by the more enlightened members of the audience:

"Poor chap, they've both ganged up on him . . ."

". . . he was a perfect gentleman when Johnny was ill".

But it was when the butcher's young widow broke ranks and came over to me saying quietly that if I went to her flat just around the corner she could treat my black eye with a raw steak, that I decided the performance had ended and a quick exit was indicated.

Gathering my few possessions I jumped into the car and drove off to my main clinic where I arrived an hour later and locked myself and my belongings in the doctors' toilet. This was such a narrow slit of a room that half its width was taken up by the pocket-sized washbasin, which protruded from its side wall. If the door was not wide open, it was impossible, even sideways, to squeeze in or out, because the edge of the door only just cleared the edge of the washbasin. I undressed completely and proceeded to shave. Then considering it my duty, I did my best to take a bath in the petite washbasin, no doubt making peculiar thumping and splashing noises. Soon one of my clinic nurses was knocking at the door asking in a frightened voice if I was all right. On being assured I was, she went away. By now the floor of the small lavatory was swimming with soapy water which was seeping under the door into the corridor outside. I was standing on one leg on the lid of the lavatory pan, trying to dry one of my feet, when I lost my balance and crashed to the floor in a tangle of arms and legs. Then came authoritative knocks on the door, accompanied by the unmistakable deep contralto voice of my good friend the Chief Nursing Officer, enquiring if I needed any help! I told her that everything was under control and that I would see her for coffee in half an hour. After a complete change of clothing and with my discarded clothes under both arms, I managed to unlock the lavatory door and as I stepped into the corridor, I collided with two cleaners with mops and buckets attending to the minor flood which was beginning to seep under the doors of the adjacent rooms. They gave me a withering look as I left with my black eye to dump my unwanted paraphernalia in the car.

Knowing that I could trust the Chief Nursing Officer with any professional confidences, my only problem was to explain the puffy purple mass surrounding the slit between my swollen eyelids. After outlining the smallpox saga I came to the part, that as a woman she most wanted to hear, and I think I carried it off.

"You see last night my wallet had dropped onto the floor of the car and though I had pulled up, I had forgotten to put the light on, and in ducking down quickly in the pitch dark to pick it up from the passenger side, the knob on top of the gear stick landed me a straight left to the right eye!"

At least she didn't suggest raw steak but she did insist on a pad and bandage for my eye in case patients got the wrong idea. The morning passed uneventfully and after lunch I set off to meet the Major-General. I'd met a few Air Vice-Marshals and Rear Admirals and they were quite normal, but I'd met only one Major-General and he'd had so many plums in his mouth that all I could hear when he deigned to speak was 'Wah! Wah! Wah! What?' However, this afternoon's Major-General was quite a wise old boy who looked knowingly at me when I said I ran an amateur boxing club. After taking a careful history and performing a thorough examination he stated that the young girl did not have smallpox. She was suffering from an atypical form of papulo-vesicular erythema multiforme, a disease which was beginning to cause increasing confusion in the differential diagnosis of smallpox, especially since these diseases may give similar blood test results. But most importantly she was going to recover and there was no danger of anyone catching it from her. The relief was overwhelming for the parents, and by teatime the episode was closed – or was it?

I still had to remember it was only my wife and mother who knew the whole story, including the cause of the black eye, and that my senior professional colleagues were privy to the smallpox story but not to the black eye, whereas our neighbours had been told that my car had broken down but had been repaired. It was the clothes-throwing, and the things that were said during the impromptu ballet performance, witnessed by so many parents and children, that we found difficult to explain. Our story, that because my car had broken down I was very late for an important meeting at the Welsh Office a hundred miles away and needed a rapid change of clothing, didn't ring true; and months later we were surprised to receive telephone calls from various families of close friends living in different parts of the country, making kindly but thinly veiled enquiries about our health and happiness.

From a personal point of view it would have been less traumatic to have acted out most of the scenes on the open stage; but from the public standpoint it was wiser to have kept the curtains closed.

PHAROAH OR TERRORIST?

It was a balmy autumn morning many years ago when I received that call from a doctor in general practice, asking me if I would visit a patient of his he thought might have smallpox. Nowadays, as a result of the application of the principles of public health medicine, the world is free of that revolting disease, but at the time I received the call, a diagnosis of fulminating smallpox was tantamount to a death warrant. He told me that the patient was a three-year-old boy who had not been vaccinated against smallpox because he suffered from asthma. The child and his parents were Egyptian, and had recently arrived from Egypt. I couldn't help recalling that Rameses V, King of Egypt, had died of smallpox in 1160 BC when he was forty years old. The child's father was a university student living with his wife and son in a flat on the overseas campus of the college, with about a hundred other overseas students and their families, most from countries where smallpox was endemic.

It was therefore considered wise in the circumstances to proceed exactly as laid down in the rulebook, especially as regards clothing to be worn by doctors while examining a patient with suspected smallpox. This entails the removal of some outer clothing, and then the donning of an operating theatre gown closely fitting around the neck and tied at the back like a shroud, together with white Wellington boots whose tops are covered by the long gown. To cap it all, one wears a one-piece all-over hat and mask completely covering the head, neck and face, except for a narrow slit for the eyes, so that the overall appearance is rather like that of a member of the SAS, and the doctor has to rely on the kindness of his voice to assuage the understandable apprehension of the patient and relatives. Our difficulty was to decide where to change, as we could hardly change in the hospital and drive through town wearing the appropriate garb and, in any event, driving a car in Wellington boots, even without a bank robber's headgear, is not to be recommended. So we decided to commandeer a room in the flat we were to visit, as a changing room.

When we arrived in convoy at the site, I was somewhat disconcerted to see small knots of African and Asiatic students with their families, grouped around lamp posts. They were eyeing us with a certain degree of suspicion, tinged with fear. As we drove slowly through the campus, more and more people appeared and I noticed a small crowd had gathered around one block of flats in the centre of the campus. I was embarrassed to find that this was the location of the third-floor flat we were to visit, and I realized I should have asked my colleague exactly what he had said to the parents. From the graciousness of the reception I received from the bystanders, I suspected that he had billed me as an international authority on the diseases of Egyptian children (which I most certainly was not), but in fact it was simply a manifestation of the innate courtesy of these charming people.

The flat was approached by three flights of uncovered concrete steps on the outside of the block, rather like a fire escape, and was overflowing with people who were obviously friends of the family and who seemed most concerned for their welfare. The flat was so small it would have been churlish to have requisitioned a room as a changing room. So we had no alternative but to use the small open concrete platform at the top of the outside steps, and change in full view of the gathering crowd of onlookers who had not managed to get into the flat, or secure a place on one of the flights of concrete steps. It really was quite a charade and I began to feel sorry for my colleague, who was rather shy and tended to blush easily; in fact, as I found out later, he had never appeared on stage before, even at school. After pulling on long, white Wellington boots, we removed our jackets and waistcoats and gave them into the custody of an authoritative-looking Egyptian gentleman. We then donned our long operating theatre gowns and tied one another into them from behind. Fortuitously I was sheathed in a white gown, whereas my colleague was in a green one. We were fairly confident that the significance of this accidental colour distinction would be lost upon our overseas audience, but we were both cognisant of the fact that members of the highest Order of the Gorsedd of Bards of the Isle of Britain, the Druids, wear white robes, whereas members of the lowest order, the Ovates, wear green. However, we soon began to have doubts about our assumption, because after gowning-up, I was treated with the deference due to a reincarnated pharaoh accompanied by a member of his court. But the *pièce de résistance* was the covering for the face and head and neck which unfortunately was coloured black. My companion had not worn one of these before and put it on back to front so that his face was completely covered in black cloth and I fancied a murmur rose from the crowd below.

After the necessary adjustments we entered the flat and I was aware of the sudden silence that descended upon the congregation thronging the passageway. We were led to a door which was thrown open. We must have presented an awesome sight – two figures standing there in the doorway looking like a cross between surgeons about to cut open someone's heart, and active members of a central European terrorist gang. The first thing I remember was the unearthly howl let out by the wife holding the child, as she retreated behind a high-backed chair, and the sudden forward movement of the brave husband, arm raised to defend his wife and child from these hooded creatures. The child, not to be outdone by his mother, started to yell in terror, peal after peal of ear-splitting screams, interrupted only by sharp bubbling intakes of breath in order that he might produce even more piercing and penetrating shrieks, which must have reverberated around the block of flats. I was loath to think what the crowd outside imagined we were doing to this poor child and, recalling the lamp-posts in the campus, I wondered when the last public lynching had occurred. Soon the mother crumpled down behind the high-backed chair, so that the child could no longer see the two monsters in the doorway, and the father, somehow recognising the dumpy figure of his own doctor, lowered his arm. After a few minutes, the child's screams gradually gave way to a moist, blubbering whimper as he became more and more exhausted, and my colleague's soothing tones could then just be heard through the black material which was stuck to his face with sweat.

Within ten minutes the little boy was fast asleep in his mother's arms, his face red and hot with exertion and shiny with drying tears. I then obtained a detailed history from the parents, and after the mother had undressed the child, I was able to examine him without waking him up. Even the most experienced clinicians make mistakes, but especially in a case of suspected smallpox one always errs on the side of public safety. So I was a long time considering the history and my examination of the child to arrive at a clinical diagnosis, which at best can only be an informed guess. I was also very aware of the widespread adverse publicity that would surround a doctor who missed a case of smallpox. But I was as certain as I could be that this little boy had chickenpox and not smallpox, and I told the parents so. I had not bargained for the expressions of relief that overcame that little family. The father flung his arms around me in a bear hug and tried to kiss me on both cheeks, and I must admit that the sight of the tears of joy running down the cheeks of the gentle mother clasping her sleeping child to her bosom almost brought a lump to my throat.

As we were changing back into our everyday clothes, the news passed down the steps to the crowd below, like an insistent ripple making its way across the surface of an uneasy sea. The demonstrations of joy reached their climax as the charming young mother with her little boy joined me on the platform, while her husband and the doctor stood behind. For those few seconds the concrete platform had became a stately balcony and, may I be forgiven, I could not resist raising my hand in a regal wave!

When we arrived back at the hospital to return our borrowed kit, my colleague was in a great hurry as he was late for surgery and, after thanking me for my help, disappeared in a screech of tyres. I never got round to asking him what exactly he had said to that delightful couple before our visit.

THREE O'CLOCK IN THE AFTERNOON

Police enquiries had suggested that the owners of a certain ancient castle were 'recluses living in deplorable conditions'. Boys who had breached the defences of the castle and looked through the windows of the Georgian house, built on the site of the castle keep, made a terrified exit. They reported seeing a decaying human corpse sitting bolt upright in an armchair. So I was obliged to act.

The gates of the castle were securely padlocked and no one was ever admitted.

National newspapers headlined and dramatized my projected 'attack' upon the castle by referring to my '. . . laying siege to the castle, whose battlements would be manned (*sic!*) by a middle-aged lady', and predicted that, 'The attackers, led by Dr St George Rhys (*sic!*), are in for a hard fight to penetrate the stronghold.' The report continued, 'Twelve years ago when a court warrant was issued for the arrest of the owner – for non-payment of rates – the authorities failed to breach the defences to execute the warrant.'

★   ★   ★

My wife and I were moving house and it was four o'clock in the morning of that Thursday in the 1970s by the time the removals men had unloaded the last tea chest. Too exhausted to unpack after hundreds of miles of travelling we slept that first night on the bare floorboards of the house that had been empty for years. We had an intermittent flow of well water, a wavering electricity supply and no telephone. Although the men had to leave before the village shop opened, they were grateful that we were able to provide them with a substantial breakfast of curried sardines on slices of rich fruit-cake, followed by two siphon bottles of soda water.

Our morning's unpacking was interrupted by the out-of-breath vicar calling to say he'd had a telephone message from the chief administrator of the local authority area where the castle stood, over seventy miles away, stating my presence was required there as a matter of urgency. We asked him in and as he was so agitated about the 'phone call, I proceeded to explain to him over a glass of sherry-wine, as he called it, that the word 'urgent', when used by a surgeon, meant 'within minutes', but when used by a local authority officer meant 'at your earliest convenience'. He was an intellectual and we had a most interesting discussion on Pelagianism while we sat on tea-chests eating the remains of the fruit-cake.

When I eventually rang the chief administrator's office from the vicarage, his secretary confided to me that he was in a highly nervous state, had locked himself in his office and was refusing to see anyone or take any telephone calls. When I explained that it was he who wanted to speak to me and not vice versa, I was put through. The poor man was distraught, and not without reason. Apparently the media had wind that an 'attack' on the castle was imminent, and he himself was under siege from the local and national press and the BBC as well as an assortment of television companies; and excited townspeople wanted to know why so many large television and recording vans had been blocking the main road. Not for the first time did I regret the paucity of my psychiatric training for I was quite unable to calm him down. Knowing from past experience that members of my own competent, highly qualified public health staff were always only too glad to deputise for me, I reassured him that I had every faith in the two representatives I had in the town and I was in the act of putting the 'phone down when I heard an agonised high-pitched cry, as of an animal in pain, coming out of the earpiece. He begged me to come down in person to execute the Court Warrant of Entry timed for three o'clock that very afternoon. He said that because of the intense media interest, it would be appropriate if I, as statutory head of the department, appeared. There were other, darker aspects. The owner's aged mother had not been heard of for many years and some time ago two boys on a window-breaking spree had reported seeing her decaying body sitting bolt upright in an armchair. Many local people considered the owner, Miss Scratton, should be put in an old people's home and her mother's remains given a decent burial. All this came as a considerable shock because I had always managed to sidestep the limelight, so much so that my nickname in the local press was 'The Scarlet Pimpernel'. However, this time there was no way out. Only a few hours left and I couldn't remember where I'd packed my shaving tackle.

★ ★ ★

It had all started some five months previously when Miss Scratton had written to the police complaining that youths were breaking into the castle grounds and throwing stones at the windows of her house. Incidentally, the construction of the house was commenced during the Regency period on the site of the castle keep and later the house passed into the hands of the High Sheriff. Miss Scratton and her mother had moved there before the Second World War. Enquiries had indicated that Miss Scratton and her aged mother were living the lives of recluses in deplorable conditions. The authorities were informed and I was asked, as the Medical Officer of Health, to investigate. In my letter of explanation to Miss Scratton I proposed visiting her on a specific date at 3 o'clock in the afternoon to see if I could help in any way. She denied receiving this letter. Unfortunately I developed influenza and was obliged to send a telegram, 'Visit postponed. Letter follows. Dr Rhys'. This telegram was taken to the police who advised Miss Scratton to take it to the post office, whereupon the headquarters of GPO Telegrams contacted me to say Miss Scratton stated the telegram was not for her. I was advised in future to send all letters to her by recorded delivery.

My next letter was delivered by recorded delivery but the postmaster was obliged to sign confirming delivery, as Miss Scratton had refused to sign. In that letter, again explaining the reasons for my visit, I proposed calling one month later also at 3 o'clock in the afternoon. Miss Scratton chose to reply, neither to myself nor to the chief administrator of her area, but sent a splendid fighting letter to the chief administrator of a neighbouring area, over one hundred miles away, and he of course knew nothing of the matter. He made haste to send her letter on to me because I was, in any event, responsible for such matters. Miss Scratton still denied receiving my first letter and astounded the blameless recipient of her letter by asking:

'Is this some new form of official trickery, or is it, as I am convinced, the second stage of a hoax which began last month when a telegram arrived which simply said, 'Visit postponed. Letter follows. Dr Rhys'. Apparently this man has an official address but it is most suspicious and irregular. Stationery can be stolen or forged. We are not members of the Health Service. Officialdom, by its very nature, has to state its business in writing and is supplied with every available form for this purpose. It does not behave like this man – announcing to astonished strangers that he is coming or not coming as the case may be.'

To his credit the chief administrator replied stating that I was 'a very reasonable person'. It was becoming obvious that 'The Chatelaine of the Castle', as I later found she liked to be known, was going to have no truck with anyone of my ilk, which of course made me more determined to visit her as arranged, and so I assembled my troops consisting of a justice of the peace, one of my health visitors, one of my public health inspectors, my senior welfare officer and his assistant, together with two members of the police force.

At precisely 3 o'clock in the afternoon as stated in my letter we arrived at the iron gates of the ruined castle on top of the rocky ridge dominating the town and river. The gates were securely padlocked, and we were obliged to descend outside the massive stone walls to the level of the river and we began to circumnavigate the curtain wall. Eventually we found a small entrance gap and entered the grounds where we encountered what can only be described as a mass of practically infrangible boscage. We fought our way up through this almost impenetrable undergrowth and at last, with bleeding hands and torn clothes, arrived at a large semicircular clearing in front of an imposing but decaying Georgian house. Its broken, shuttered windows looked out despairingly at us while I punished the huge brass doorknocker whose echoes reverberated within the house. Though we could hear movements inside the house, no one answered our repeated loud knockings. Our expedition brought forth another brilliant letter from Miss Scratton to the chief administrator of the neighbouring authority:

'On Tuesday 17ᵗʰ at 3pm a crowd of people turned up and hammered on our front door knocker for twenty minutes (I timed it). They were not invited and they were not received. Their manner of entry was most suspicious. They avoided our main front gates where they would have been under the scrutiny of adjacent offices, sneaked in over a wire fence and broke open a side garden door which was securely fastened. They left by the same route. I am glad that I contacted you otherwise we could not have believed this nasty ambush was conceived and carried out by the Medical Officer of Health. The activities of government are generally viewed with distrust, but this sequence of events really takes the biscuit.'

My third letter to Miss Scratton again gave chapter and verse explaining the purpose of my next proposed visit two weeks hence at 3 o'clock in the afternoon. This time I was the one honoured with her reply, which again was in true indomitable spirit:

'The suggested appointment date will NOT be convenient. You came here on Tuesday the 17ᵗʰ in a party and you poked your noses wherever you wished to poke them, and that, as far as you are concerned, is that.'

In my fourth letter I asked Miss Scratton if she would kindly indicate which dates and times, during the next fourteen days, would be convenient for a visit. I allowed a few days for postal delays but received no reply. This left me no alternative but to commence my fifth letter ominously: 'Nineteen days have now elapsed since my letter to you of . . .' I still hoped that she would reply – but no. Miss Scratton had now refused three reasonable requests by the Medical Officer of Health for admission to her premises, and since only one refusal was stipulated under the relevant Act of Parliament, it became necessary to obtain a Warrant of Entry to the premises and the Warrant was duly issued. Although the law comes down heavily on the sort of intransigence shown by Miss Scratton, and although she was in fact becoming a confounded nuisance to me, there was a strand in her attitude of defiance that I was secretly beginning to admire. However, it now became my statutory duty to ensure that the Court Warrant was duly executed. The date and time were fixed for twenty-one days hence at 3 o'clock in the afternoon and Miss Scratton was accordingly notified that the Warrant would be executed, if need be by force, on the date and at the time specified.

⋆　⋆　⋆

After recoiling from the shock of the chief administrator's revelations to me at the vicarage that Thursday morning, I had only a few hours to make arrangements to cover eventualities; for example, if I found that the aged mother was in fact alive but was ill and living in insanitary conditions and not being properly looked after, I could, with the agreement of a court, have her removed to a hospital or old people's home in seven days time, unless she agreed to voluntary removal. If, however, I considered she required immediate removal and she refused, then I needed to have another doctor, a justice of the peace and one of my welfare officers on the spot there and then, together with the promise of a bed for her, in order for my welfare officer to effect her immediate removal.

Alternatively I might just need an undertaker.

The vicar kindly allowed me to use his telephone and I persuaded another doctor and a justice of the peace to be there at 3 o'clock that afternoon, and also told my public health inspectors and welfare officers that I might well require their assistance. The police had already been informed.

I drove the seventy-six miles to the chief administrator's office, but failed to persuade him to join the party. My colleagues who were waiting in my local office suggested we walk rather than drive the few hundred yards to the castle gates. My doctor colleague who, like me, had never seen the castle gates unlocked, asked me if I had arranged for a locksmith to be in attendance. Just before three o'clock, the seven of us attempted to thread our way inconspicuously in single file through the crowds, hoping no one would be aware of our mission. But Miss Scratton had informed the media and unfortunately our intentions had been headlined in the national and local press as well as having been announced on radio and television. It was a vain hope, not helped by the fact that one of our party was ostentatiously wielding a full-sized crowbar and another was sporting an authentic jemmy and other implements used in forcible entry. By the time we reached the castle gates we found we were at the head of a phalanx of vocal and excited people. This was indeed party time. We found the gates open and I could sense the disappointment in my crowbar-jemmy-swinging colleagues, so I encouraged them saying that it was likely there were obstructions ahead.

However, I was utterly nonplussed to be confronted with a huge television camera mounted on a wide movable carriage almost completely blocking the way in. The cameraman with his spiky purple hair and a saffron-coloured shirt, was perched high up on the contraption like a queen-bee above a swarm of equally queer-looking workers, droning around the entrance. Out of the kaleidoscopic mishmash of indigo, green and

232

crimson hair fashioned in peculiar styles with matching nose-rings and ear-rings, vividly coloured shirts and shimmering scarves, a soberly dressed man in a black cape, who seemed to be in charge, emerged and asked for me by name.

He said, "I want you to march resolutely down the drive to the castle, chin up, teeth clenched, breathing fire followed by your retinue brandishing their weapons." Thinking he was joking I asked him if he would also like us to wear make-up, stetsons and black eye-patches, but realising he was serious, I told him to clear off. As I walked down the drive the camera-on-wheels preceded me, its huge eye glinting at me in the afternoon sunlight. It was then I noticed that there were other cameras and microphones accompanying me, but I was disappointed to see that my party had fallen back so that I was now alone and well ahead of them. There was a sprinkling of onlookers on both sides of the drive, but when I reached the semicircular clearing in front of the house, I found that my colleagues had melted away into the crowds of people jostling for position at the perimeter of the area, while the police held them back.

It was at that moment when I felt deserted, left standing, a solitary figure in the centre of this large open space, that a feeling of indignation welled up inside me. I was a doctor, a qualified surgeon. What in the hell was I doing here? And then it came to me. This was live theatre. I had an eager audience and I must not let them down. The parts I had usually been called upon to play in amateur productions were those of a scatty professor or a bumbling vicar, but this was very different. Two reporters with microphones crept up to me. I brushed them aside. The beautiful Georgian house, which must at one time have been as delightful as any in the county, now stood silent, blinkered. It was a sorry sight. There was no glass in the ground floor windows and all the shutters were closed and, as if for some added protection, a few boards had been nailed to the window frames in a haphazard manner. Even on this glorious spring afternoon the house bore an aura of foreboding, as though it held a hideous secret within its walls. I had the vision of a corpse rigid in an armchair, its long white hair still growing, thin tendrils creeping out from under the door of a locked room. Dismissing this gruesome image, it took me a few seconds to realize that the crowd had become completely silent.

The overture had ended.

It was curtain-up and I was alone centre-stage.

I must act.

Bracing my shoulders I advanced to the massive double doors, raised the heavy brass knocker once, twice, three times. The deep booming echoes seemed to resonate ominously inside the gloomy house longer than they should, followed by an uncanny silence. Not knowing the protocol on such occasions, I devised my own and, waiting for half a minute or so, I repeated the exercise twice more, but with no response. It had now got to the stage of forcible entry. It would require a battering ram to break down the heavy doors and I was contemplating another mode of entry when, hearing a gasp from the crowd, I saw that everyone was looking up, and there on the balcony above the front doors was a hooded figure.

As much of the face as was visible was chalk white, the lips and hood scarlet; the body seemed to be clothed in a scarlet cloak clasped at the throat. The contrast between the vivid scarlet of the lips and the dead matt-white of the face was so unnatural that I recalled my gibe about make-up to the television johnny at the front gate. It had to be Miss Scratton and in this performance she was firmly cast in the star role.

In an imperious voice she asked, "Where is the man Rhys?"

Returning to centre stage with my back to the audience, I entered into the spirit of the charade to the whirring of the cameras. Holding on high the Warrant, I said in my best Shakespearean voice, "Behold, I am he. In my hand I hold the Court Warrant to enter this house."

Advancing to the rail of the balcony, she raised her cloaked arm and pointing directly down at me, declaimed, "You, Dr Rhys, are the villain of the piece."

Wishing I possessed the ability to answer spontaneously in like manner, I kicked away the two tape-recorders that had been surreptitiously placed at my feet and, brushing away the woolly microphone that had appeared in front of me, I merely said, "I hereby give you one last chance. I will raise your doorknocker three times again. If you still refuse to allow me into this house, entry will be forced."

Looking over my head and addressing the assembled multitude with a majestic sweep of her cloaked right arm and in a voice charged with emotion that would have done credit to Dame Sybil Thorndike, she uttered one word:

"Never!"

Receiving no response to my final pounding of her door knocker, and considering it a shame to attack the grand front doors, yet a disgrace if we had to retreat having failed to force entry, I summoned my crowbar-jemmy-wielding assistants. They used their hefty wooden-handled slashers with vigorous enthusiasm, and cut through the dense undergrowth until we eventually reached the back of the house, where we found a door which was a burglar's delight. We soon had it down and were just stepping over it into the dark house, when one of the reporters appeared and told us Miss Scratton would prefer me to enter via the front doors, 'because it would look better'. I agreed with him that a battering-ram entry would make more exciting pictures for the newspapers and television, but told him we didn't possess one.

"No! No! Miss Scratton is now willing to open the front doors," he said.

At the front doors Miss Scratton told me, "I will allow only *you* to enter."

I insisted that I be accompanied by a female and I gave her the choice of either the justice of the peace or the police sergeant. She chose the latter and no sooner were we over the threshold than the great doors clanged shut behind us and we were in absolute darkness. I took three steps forward and went flying through the air, landing flat on my face. I raised my head and, from the dark recesses of the house, appeared an apparition carrying a candelabrum with seven lighted candles. Like something out of an Edgar Allan Poe story it advanced upon me with dishevelled white hair trailing over the shoulders. It smiled through broken yellow teeth and I heard a cracked voice saying, "So the leopard got you!"

In the total darkness I had caught my foot in the wide-open jaws of a leopard's head which was part of a leopard-skin rug, and the bearer of the guttering candles was Miss Scratton's mother; so whose corpse had the boys seen?

Mrs Scratton told her daughter, "Put them in the music room," and we were ushered into a large, square, shuttered and candlelit room to the right of the hall and in the front of the house. Miss Scratton and her mother sat on either side of the empty grate while my chaperone and I were motioned to sit on an unusually long antique sofa facing the marble fireplace. When I sat down at the other end of the sofa from the young woman police sergeant, she was propelled into my lap because my weight had driven the whole of my end of the sofa deep down through the floorboards, flaky with dry rot. Not one of us uttered a word. The silence was punctuated by intermittent crunching noises as my end of the sofa sank deeper and deeper into the void beneath the rotten floorboards, and also by the ripping sound of ancient, friable velvet upholstery being torn apart, as my chaperone, bravely clutching her arm of the sofa, was trying to heave her ample behind out of my lap. As my eyes gradually became accommodated to the dim light, a white concert grand piano took shape in one corner of the room. I became even more disorientated because the whole piano was tilted to the left, where its legs had gone through the floorboards, while the sofa was sinking to the right. Embarrassed by the continuing silence I said the first thing that came into my head, "White concert grands are rare," and I tiptoed gingerly towards it.

No one said anything. By the light of one candle and one night-light stuck in saucers on either side of the sloping keyboard I saw the Noel Coward Song Book propped up on the piano. Thinking it might possibly be a tactful move, I applauded the fact that he had been knighted. The effect was instantaneous. Mother and daughter clapped their hands and agreed wholeheartedly, and I felt that they might now begin to regard me as almost human. Building on this minor breakthrough I felt I too should respond wholeheartedly to the mother's request, "Do please play."

There was no piano stool so, kneeling at the tilting keyboard, I began to play 'Mad Dogs and Englishmen' on the hopelessly out of tune instrument. By the time I'd reached the chorus with its incomprehensible twaddle, mother and daughter were either side of the piano and the three of us were bellowing and screeching the meaningless gibberish of the chorus, 'Papalaka

papalaka papalaka boo', the mother keeping time waving her seven candles around spattering hot candle grease in all directions. Meanwhile the woman police sergeant had her head on her knees and, when we started murdering the refrain of 'A Room with a View', she left the room and sat on the stairs in the dark. After we had given raucous renditions of a selection of the songs in the book with frequent reprises, mother and daughter were most co-operative, and to use Miss Scratton's expression in one of her letters to me, I was allowed to poke my nose wherever I wanted to poke it. During my tour of the house I asked for a hammer and some nails and was able to mend and replace the door we had broken down. After a cup of extremely strong tea, we made our way to the front doors where my chaperone, no doubt thinking she had been in the company of the mentally disturbed, fled. Mother and daughter insisted on my joining them for a succession of photo calls and, when Miss Scratton asked her mother if I might be invited to call again, the reply came, "Yes, in strawberry time."

When I told my colleagues that no action was required in this case, I had the impression that they were looking rather strangely at me. Apparently our musical performance had caused most of the audience to leave, although some of the media people had tried, fortunately unsuccessfully, to record it. Time had passed so quickly that I was very surprised to read in the press that I had spent over an hour in the house.

Some years later I received an urgent request to call again – but that's another story.